THE PRIMORDIAL LAWS OF CREATION
Keys to Joyous Achievement
of Life's Purposes

Also by
STEPHEN M. LAMPE

The Christian and Reincarnation

Building Future Societies: The Spiritual Principles

Thinking About God: Reflections on Conceptions and Misconceptions

THE PRIMORDIAL LAWS OF CREATION
Keys to Joyous Achievement of Life's Purposes

STEPHEN M. LAMPE

Millennium Press
Ibadan, Nigeria

Published by Millennium Press
25, Moremi Street,
New Bodija
Ibadan
P. O. Box 38632, General Post Office,
Ibadan, Nigeria

First Published 2017

© Stephen M. Lampe

All rights reserved.
With the exception of short excerpts for reviews, no part of this publication may be reproduced, stored in a retrieval system or transmitted in any form or by any means, electronic, mechanical, photocopying, recording or otherwise without the prior permission in writing of the author and the copyright owner.

ISBN: 978-978-2751-08-9

As the inexorable and adamantine Laws in Creation operate vitally and automatically, with a power against which human spirits are entirely helpless, it stands to reason that the most urgent need of every human being must be the *thorough recognition* of these laws, to the effects of which he remains absolutely defenceless in every respect. (Abd-ru-shin *In the Light of Truth, The Grail Message*, Lecture: "The Worship of God")

Man can only make use of the powers that bear the Will of God when he studies them exactly, thus recognising them and adapting himself to them. To reckon with or adapt oneself to them really means nothing less than to adjust oneself to them, thus to submit oneself to them! It means not to go *against* these powers, but to go *with them*! Only when man adapts his will to the special nature of these powers, thus going in the same direction, can he make use of the might of these powers. (Abd-ru-shin *In the Light of Truth, The Grail Message*, Lecture: "Symbolism in the Fate of Man")

Contents

PREFACE	1
CHAPTER ONE The Idea of Primordial Laws	5
CHAPTER TWO The Law of Movement	23
CHAPTER THREE The Law of Attraction of Homogeneous Species	43
CHAPTER FOUR The Law of Reciprocal Action	61
CHAPTER FIVE The Law of Reciprocal Action and the Matter of Forgiveness	81
CHAPTER SIX The Law of Gravitation	101
CHAPTER SEVEN The Law of Balance	107
CHAPTER EIGHT The Law of the Cycle	121
CHAPTER NINE Concluding Remarks	125
INDEX	131

Preface

The best manufacturers provide manuals for their various machines. Such manuals are to ensure that the machines are used as designed and for the maximum benefit of the buyer. Wise purchasers take time to study such manuals. And in doing so they know that they are not doing the manufacturer a favour; rather the effort is entirely for their own benefit. On the other hand, to ignore the manual for a given piece of equipment out of carelessness, indolence, or for any other reasons is to deny oneself the benefits of the equipment and possibly to forgo the purposes for which one purchased the equipment.

The Creation in which all creatures have their existence was designed and developed by the Creator so that they may all achieve specific purposes ordained for their existence in whichever part of Creation they find themselves. Built into Creation is a "manual" to facilitate for all creatures attainment of their individual and collective purposes. We human beings are creatures in Creation and have a duty to be aware of, study, and understand the "manual" provided by the Creator. As with earthly manufacturers' manuals, the endeavour to study, understand and adjust to the dictates of the "manual" is exclusively for our benefits; we would not thereby be doing the Creator any favour.

The Primordial Laws of Creation, the subject of this book, are in a sense the manual that the Creator has branded into Creation and which work automatically. They indicate the paths we must follow on earth as well as in other parts of Creation and provide the foundation for the explanations of all life's mysteries. Recognition of these Primordial Laws is the most urgent need for all of us human beings, especially in these increasingly uncertain and tumultuous times. These Laws transcend religion and they impact everyone automatically, regardless of belief or unbelief. Therefore, to study and apply them is simply to tread the path of wisdom.

I should stress that the Laws of Creation apply not just to individuals but also to groups, whether small or large. They apply to corporations and should be the foundation of corporate ethics and corporate behaviour, just as they should guide the constitutions and political structures of countries and nation-states. Indeed, governance and public policy-making should follow the dictates of the Primordial Laws of Creation in all sectors — social, economic, and political. The relationships among ethnic and racial groups within and across countries must adapt to the Primordial Laws of Creation; otherwise sustained harmony is impossible.

When we as individuals adjust ourselves to the Primordial Laws in thought, word, deed, and in our general attitude to life we get the full backing of all the forces and mechanisms in Creation as we go through life. Such backing ensures happiness, harmonious relationships, lasting accomplishments and inner contentment. And even more important, we are guaranteed joyful automatic ascent to our spiritual home where we would live eternally. If we ignore the Primordial Laws of Creation, we arraign all the forces of Creation against us and continually invite disharmony, chaos, and failures in all aspects of human existence.

Stephen M. Lampe
July 21, 2017

CHAPTER ONE
The Idea of Primordial Laws

The expression, "Primordial Laws of Creation", which is the title of this book, ought to be familiar to all of us because they affect everybody constantly and inevitably. "Primordial", in the sense in which it is used here, describes what existed from the very beginning of time. Thus, the Primordial Laws of Creation are laws that were associated with the coming into being of Creation, laws that were already in place at the very beginning of Creation. We can right away infer that whatever came into existence at the very beginning of Creation must have come through the action of the Creator, God.

The inference is correct for, indeed, the Primordial Laws of Creation are activated by the Power of God and constitute the Will of God. The development of Creation, including the coming into existence of all the invisible and visible worlds and creatures therein, followed the pattern (or blueprint) dictated by the Primordial Laws. It follows that we human beings, as creatures in Creation, are inextricably connected and subject to these Primordial Laws. Therefore, wisdom dictates that we become intimately familiar with them and adjust to their dictates.

Closely associated with the Realm of God is the Divine Realm, which came into existence as an inevitable consequence of the eternal and unceasing radiation of God. The Divine Realm has, therefore, always existed and it is *not* a product of a willed Act of Creation. In other words, the Divine Realm already existed at the very beginning; thus, the Primordial Laws of Creation may also be called the Divine Laws of Creation. Because these laws are eternal, they may be described as The Eternal Laws.

It is obvious that the Primordial Laws of Creation by their very origin and nature can be *comprehensively* known only by those who existed at the very beginning. Creatures in Subsequent Creation, such as earthmen, may recognize fragments of the Primordial Laws only if they strive strenuously to observe everything around them in the right way. But they can only be known in their comprehensiveness through revelation.

This revelation, along with other spiritual knowledge, came through Abd-ru-shin (whose civil name was Oskar Ernst Bernhardt) in his unique work "*In the Light of Truth*", *The Grail Message*. What I present here represents in a sense an oversimplification of the subject — only my own limited understanding of the work whose depth and scope are so stupendous that it would be foolish for anyone to claim complete understanding of it. Therefore, those seriously interested in this subject, and in spiritual knowledge generally, should endeavour to study Abd-ru-shin's work and should not be content with the understanding of another person. I consider the work as the Alpha and Omega of spiritual knowledge[1].

If we regard Creation as one gigantic computer one may, as a crude analogy, say that the Primordial Laws are its operating system. A computer program indicates the intentions and plan of the programmer; in an analogous manner, the Primordial Laws express the intentions and plan of the Creator. Only those functions that are allowed for in a computer program can be executed. In a similar sense, only what are inherent in the Primordial Laws of Creation can flourish and be sustained. Attempts at carrying out activities not permitted by the Laws must come to grief and are guaranteed ultimately to fail.

In connection with this crude analogy, let me immediately state that it is impossible

---

[1] Abd-ru-shin, *In the Light of Truth, The Grail Message.* Vomperberg, Tyrol, Alexander Bernhardt Publishing Co., 1979. 3 volumes.

to interfere with the Primordial Laws, unlike human computer systems that can be hacked, tampered with, and distorted. Moreover, unlike any computer system, the Primordial Laws of Creation are perfect and cannot be improved upon.

To appreciate the scope of our subject, we should note the vastness of the Creation that is maintained by these Laws. Our earth is only a planet in the solar system, a system built around the sun, and the sun is only one of the *billions* of stars in our galaxy, the Milky Way. The Milky Way galaxy is in turn only one of *billions* of galaxies in our Universe. The size of the known physical universe as well as the complex and great speeds of the motions of its members are simply mind-boggling. Thus, it becomes obvious that the earth, with its various types of inhabitants, is no more than a tiny speck in the *known* universe.

And the known universe itself is only a part of the World of Gross Matter, which is situated at the outermost periphery of what we loosely call Creation. As a matter of fact, the World of Matter is only a *consequence* of the actual Creation; it is not part of original Creation. For this reason, the material world is appropriately designated as a part of Subsequent Creation. The World of Matter constitutes only a very small part of what came into being as a consequence of the actual Creation by the Act of God. The actual Creation is spiritual and it is everlasting. For a further discussion of Creation and Subsequent Creation, reference may be made to Chapter 5 of the book *Thinking About God: Reflections on Conceptions and Misconceptions*[2].

The reality is such that nothing in the whole of Creation can ignore the Creation-wide Primordial Laws without dire and deleterious consequences. Indeed, everything adjusts to them as a matter of course; unfortunately, human beings on earth are the exception. On account of their misuse of their Free Will, they have for millennia unwisely attempted to ignore these laws and to embrace only the laws of their own making. In our time, the entire world is witnessing to varying degrees of intensity the dire effects of the ignorance of the Primordial Laws and of disregarding them wittingly and unwittingly.

Foundation for Sustainable Progress

Bertrand Russell (1872-1970) was a remarkable individual. He was a renowned philosopher, logician, mathematician, and a

---

[2] Stephen M. Lampe, *Thinking About God: Reflections on Conceptions and Misconceptions*, Ibadan, Millennium Press, 2014.

prolific writer of essays and books on a wide variety of philosophical, social, and political issues. In 1950, he was awarded the Nobel Prize for Literature "in recognition of his many-sided and important work in which he has constantly stood forth as a champion of humanity and freedom of thought". In an essay he first published in 1929 in the book entitled *Marriage and Morals* Russell wrote:

> The desire to understand the world and the desire to reform it are the two great engines of progress, without which human society would stand still or retrogress.[3]

The two desires to understand and to reform are, indeed, absolutely important and many who have made lasting positive impact on their societies or the world at large have been impelled by them. But, of course, mere desires are not sufficient; they must be associated with appropriate actions. In these times, humanity is beset with innumerable problems and perplexities. Attempts using various approaches to solve these problems have been made and are being made by numerous individuals, groups, societies, and governments around the world. The lack of success is evident from the current state of

---

[3] Robert E. Egner and Lester E. Denonn, editors. *The Basic Writings of Bertrand Russell 1903-1959*, New York, Simon and Schuster, 1967, p. 356.

the world. The need to understand the world and the necessity for reforms are greater and more urgent today than ever.

These problems and perplexities have a spiritual root. The efforts that have hitherto been made and are being made may be likened to polishing and shining the armour of a dying knight while leaving the knight himself untreated. Obviously, the priority should be to treat the knight who could then personally arrange to shine his armour once he has regained his health. Knowledge of the spiritual nature of the human being, the purpose of human existence, the eternal principles by which human beings should live, and genuine commitment to such principles constitute the medicine for humanity's multifarious ailments.

The Primordial Laws of Creation are the eternal principles by which we should always have lived and by which we must live. I am convinced that the Primordial Laws of Creation constitute both the infallible basis for a comprehensive understanding of the world and the sure foundation for all right reforms for all sectors. Without the knowledge and application of these laws, we would continue to walk into the embrace of retrogression and perhaps catastrophic collapse.

General Comments on the Primordial Laws

The Will of God is universal, encompassing the entire Creation, visible and invisible. Rightly understood, it does not depend on religion and it is the same for everybody — theists, atheists, agnostics, and the indifferent. The Will of God is expressed in eternal, immutable, and universal spiritual principles, which are designated Primordial Spiritual Laws. They are the perfect mechanism by which God relates to Creation and all creatures. The Laws have existed since eternity, as already stated; indeed, Creation and Subsequent Creation including human spirits came into, and can remain in, existence only through the operation of these laws.

The commandments given through prophets of various religions are essentially explanations of what we should do in order to conform to the Laws that express the Will of God. The Primordial Laws of Creation are like the manual of instructions, which we should study and follow strictly to ensure that the mechanisms in Creation serve us and lead us towards a joyful life and the achievement of the purpose of our existence.

Therefore, it is wrong to think that we do God a favour by obeying His laws or commandments; just as we do not do a manufacturer any favour when we study and follow the operating manual of a piece of equipment. The commandments of God "are in reality nothing but an explanation of the Divine Will which has been resting in Creation from the very beginning, and which cannot be circumvented by a hair's breadth!" (*In the Light of Truth, The Grail Message*, Volume II, Lecture: "I am the Lord thy God!").

On account of God's perfection, His Will is perfect and, therefore, the Primordial Laws that manifest this Will are also perfect. They cannot be improved upon, and they remain absolutely unchangeable. Therefore, we simply must seek to understand and apply these Laws, and not imagine that we can come up with different principles that can work equally well. We human beings are only products of these Laws; therefore, there can be no question of our improving on them. Indeed, we can achieve lasting success only to the degree of our adjustment to the Primordial Laws of Creation. When individuals or groups deviate from these Laws, they invite chaos and confusion, as is the case today in much of the world.

God bears all the Laws within Him in the purest form and, therefore, will never act in a manner contrary to these Laws. All of God's actions can only be in complete harmony with the Laws of Creation in the forms applicable in each part of Creation. The Lord Jesus Christ, of course, knew this; like God, Jesus could only act in accordance with the Primordial Laws of Creation. For this reason, He said that He had not come to overthrow the laws. But He did reinterpret the Mosaic laws to bring them closer to what the Primordial Laws of Creation prescribe.

The Laws apply equally to all, regardless of personal circumstances or beliefs. The effects of the Laws are the same on those who know them as well as on those who don't or choose to ignore them. Ignorance is neither excuse nor bliss!

It should be noted that the laws of nature or the laws of science are simply the gross material, earthly *forms* of the Primordial Laws of Creation. In other words, any scientific law that is correct must necessarily conform to the Primordial Laws of Creation. If a scientific law were to contradict a Law of Creation, such a scientific "law" would eventually be found to be wrong!

Thus, the best efforts of science can only discover fragments of the earthly manifestations of the Primordial Laws of Creation. Since science can successfully probe only what is material, it is forever precluded from a comprehensive knowledge of the Primordial Laws of Creation. And there is no question of its ever discovering the origin of these Laws.

It is necessary to stress that the same basic laws apply in all sections of Creation and Subsequent Creation. And the effects are uniform within each species of Creation. However, the effects of the laws are influenced differently by different species of Creation. Thus, the manifestations of each of the Laws of Creation on earth will be different from their manifestations in the immediate Beyond and in the Spiritual Realm. The manifestations of the laws in the world of thoughts would differ somewhat from their manifestations in visible, tangible matter but they are uniform in both worlds.

From this fact, it can be surmised that as science, especially specialties like quantum physics, reach into fine and finer gross matter, it may encounter changes in the *forms* in which the laws of nature express themselves. Indeed, it can be said that the indication that science is probing into a different subspecies of Gross Matter is the fact of a change in the *form* in which well-known natural laws manifest themselves.

Primordial Laws Contrasted with Human-Made Laws

For a deeper understanding of the nature of the Primordial Laws, let us contrast them with the laws that human beings make. The latter are the products of imperfect human beings and are, therefore, far from being perfect. And being imperfect, they continually need to be adjusted to changing circumstances, unlike the Primordial Laws, which are immutable. The changes to human-made laws could be so substantial that what was perfectly legal yesterday could be criminalized today. Moreover, it can be said that the best human-made laws can lead to the right means, but not to the *ends*, of human existence.

Unlike the Laws of Creation that are the same everywhere, human-made laws vary from society to society. And they are generally difficult to understand. Therefore, we depend, for their interpretation, on lawyers who have devoted many years to their study. And even lawyers do not always agree on the interpretation of a given law. In contrast, the Primordial Laws of Creation that express the Will of God are simple, clear, and easy to understand. No schooling, in the ordinary sense of the word, is required to understand them. In fact, they are hinted at in the proverbs of even relatively primitive cultures.

The Primordial Laws take fully into account thoughts, motives, and volitions in addition to actions and words of human beings. Human-made laws do *not* take into account a person's thinking and subjective factors like motives. It is said that even when purporting to deal with motives, human legal systems are really only concerned with the external manifestations of motives. With human-made laws, the overriding principle is captured by the popular saying among lawyers: "it is trite law that the thought of man is not triable, for even the devil does not know what the thought of man is."

Unlike earthly judges, the servants of the Creator who uphold His Will in Creation are supremely capable of monitoring and acting on a person's thinking, motives, and volitions and ensuring appropriate consequences. Thoughts are real and do take on invisible forms; and the effects of the thought-forms eventually manifest tangibly in the visible world.

Human-made laws do not always promote justice. Indeed, quite often, they are exploited by lawyers to set free people who have actually committed crimes. In contrast, the Laws of Creation ensure that, at all times, Justice and Love are simultaneously upheld. With human-made laws, legality and morality are separate matters. There are cases of human-made laws that are obviously unjust and hateful and yet are considered "legal".

As an example, the Supreme Court of the United States of America in 1856 ruled in the case of Dred Scott v. Sandford that slaves were the property of their owners and were not entitled to any constitutional protection. It should be recalled that the second paragraph of the United States Declaration of Independence states inter alia: "We hold these truths to be self-evident, that all men are created equal, that they are endowed by their Creator with certain unalienable Rights; that among these are Life, Liberty and the Pursuit of Happiness."

In a dissenting opinion, however, Justice John McLean wrote that a "slave is not mere chattel. He bears the impress of his Maker, and is amenable to the laws of God and man." That obnoxious Supreme Court decision is an example of the changeable nature of human-made laws, their sometimes unjust character, as well as the possibility of their inconsistent, if not irrational, interpretations.

The atrocities that Adolf Hitler's Nazi regime carried out were duly backed by so-called laws. For example, part of the Nuremberg anti-Semitic legislation of 1935 declared that German citizens of Jewish origin who were then outside the country or thereafter left it would lose their German citizenship and their property would be confiscated by the German state. During the Nazi period, such unjust and obnoxious ordinances had the full force of law. According to the doctrine of legal positivism, any ordinance made by a recognized authority of the state (such as the Nazi regime) is considered valid law.

Following the collapse of the Nazi regime, the courts of the Federal Republic of Germany repudiated legal positivism; instead they recognized the imperative to take into account principles of natural justice or the doctrine of Natural Law.

Some German physicians accused of murdering prisoners in medical experiments argued that their actions were authorized during the Nazi rule. Their defence was rejected on the grounds that the law that backed their action was against natural justice. One court concluded that "law must be defined as an ordinance or precept devised in the service of justice. Whenever the conflict between an enacted law and true justice reaches unendurable proportions, the enacted law must yield to justice, and be considered a 'lawless law'. The accused may not justify his conduct by appealing to an existing law if this law offended against certain evident principles of the natural law."[4]

Human beings make innumerable laws to govern their affairs. Given the large number of laws that societies make for themselves, it is not surprising that the laws are not always consistent and even contain contradictions. The Primordial Laws of Creation are few in number, are closely interrelated, and fully consistent. This is not surprising, since they emanate from the Executive Will of the One God. The Author of the Grail Message explains:

> For mercy and love alone are contained in the final effects of *all* the laws in Creation, which in the end rises upwards

---
[4] Cited in Charles E. Rice, *50 Questions on the Natural Law: What It Is and Why We Need It*. San Francisco, Ignatius Press, 1999, pp. 26-28

and meet in the one great basic law: The Law of Love!

Indeed, love is *everything*! Love is justice and likewise purity! There is no separation between these three. These three are one, and therein again perfection rests. Heed these my words, take them as a key for all happenings in Creation. (*In the Light of Truth, The Grail Message*, Volume III, Lecture: "Man's Spirit Guide").

To facilitate human understanding, the Primordial Laws of Creation may be discussed as the following interrelated and mutually complementary Laws: The Law of Movement; The Law of Attraction of Homogeneous Species; The Law of Reciprocal Action; The Law of Gravitation; and The Law of Balance. I will also mention briefly the Law of the Cycle, which is closely similar to the Law of Reciprocal Action.

CHAPTER TWO
The Law of Movement

All the Laws that manifest the Will of God in Creation operate within the framework of the Law of Movement. Motion is a fundamental principle throughout Creation. Even the most casual observation on earth must indicate to us the utmost significance of motion. The closer a realm is to the highest point of Creation, the more pronounced is the motion. And the further away a part of Creation is located, the more sluggish is its motion. Thus, movement in the Spiritual Realms is much more pronounced than on earth. For that reason, events and experiences that would require a thousand years to unfold on earth can be packed into one day in those realms. That is why a Bible passage states that "with the Lord one day is as a thousand years" (2 Peter 3:8).

It should be noted that the earth, similar celestial bodies, and cosmic systems are not the only objects in perpetual movement. As with the largest bodies, so it is with the smallest atomic particles; everything is in constant and uninterrupted movement. Consider a solid rock. The stationary rock is composed of chemical compounds which are themselves made up of protons, neutrons, electrons, etc., all of which are in constant movement, quite apart from the fact that the rock is being carried along in all the motions of the earth, the solar system, and the galaxy of which the earth is a part. The same can be said of the human body, dead or alive.

If a portion of a fresh, rapidly flowing river is diverted to form a stagnant pool, the pool soon loses its freshness, and may become smelly. Thus, the river maintains its freshness through movement. The hands of a boxer get bigger and stronger on account of their use. A person who exercises stays healthier than one who does not. In general, any ability that is used improves; one that is not used atrophies. All these are effects of the Law of Movement. Progress, preservation, and restoration are achieved only through movement of the right kind.

The biological principle of adaptation is a consequence of the Law of Movement. There are birds which can no longer fly because their wings have deteriorated on account of failure to use them over thousands of years. And there are fishes which are obliged to stay at the bottom of the ocean because they have lost the ability to withstand the currents.

The human spirit is subject to this same Law of Adaptation. The spiritually receptive part of the brain, the cerebellum, has become stunted relative to the intellectual part, the cerebrum, because human beings have busied themselves almost exclusively with gross material activities. Thus, we have lost most of our spiritual abilities and hardly appreciate a spiritual outlook on life. This condition is responsible for many of the problems confronting the human race, and the problems that await many in the Beyond after physical death.

The human being is subject to the Law of Movement in body, soul, and spirit. It is not sufficient to obey the Law only in so far as the physical body and earthly matters are concerned. We must also move spiritually. At present, human beings are in a way technological and intellectual giants but they are spiritual midgets; a condition that can only lead to ruin, unless a balance is restored through an accelerated development of the spirit.

The world of ideas, belief systems and religions are also subject to the Law of Movement, and consequently to the Law of Adaptation. Obedience of this Law requires that we continually and purposefully re-examine our religious and spiritual beliefs and have the courage to discard those that belong to an age and period of relative ignorance and pervasive superstition. And movement of the spirit calls for making spiritual pursuits our primary goals, with earthly goals being only secondary.

This is not difficult and does not call for queer behaviour once we know the Primordial Laws of Creation. By always acting, speaking, and thinking in ways that harmonised with those Laws, we make spiritual pursuits our primary goal. By so doing we adhere to and uphold values that are inherently noble, that promote love, justice, freedom and responsibility, and that eschew hatred and violence.

No Rigid Adherence to Questionable Beliefs

On account of the Law of Movement, one should expect that revelations from the Creator would be progressive. Therefore, we should expect new knowledge and new revelations which advance older teachings at critical periods in the development of Creation. Without new revelations, there would be stagnation and retrogression and advancement to the next higher level of spirituality and consequently of civilization would be impossible. Without the periodic infusion of new spiritual knowledge the foundations of religious beliefs would gradually collapse.

Many objective observers suspect that most religions are today in a situation of near collapse for lack of admission of new spiritual knowledge that would repair their foundations and raise their followers to the next level of spirituality and vitality. For this reason, many religious people today are believers merely out of habit and tradition; they lack real conviction in what they claim to believe.

Some people assume that it is wrong to change their religious beliefs, so they stick with the religion of their birth even when they doubt the validity of the associated beliefs. This is especially true of priests and people who hold prominent offices in their religious organizations. But they are wrong; for in accordance with the Law of Movement, one must continually re-examine one's beliefs and opinions in all matters and have the courage to change as necessary.

I have already made reference to Bertrand Russell, a Nobel Literature laureate who is regarded as one of the most outstanding philosophers and mathematicians of the twentieth Century. He was also a prominent peace activist and received awards for work on behalf of World Peace; work that included efforts to ban nuclear weapons. Robert Egner and Lester Denonn assembled some of the writings of Bertrand Russell for the period 1903 to 1959 and edited them into a volume entitled *The Basic Writings of Bertrand Russell*. In his Preface to the book, Russell wrote:

> There are things in the following collection which I wrote as long as fifty-seven years ago and which read to me now almost like the work of another person. On a very great many matters my views since I began to write on philosophy have undergone repeated changes. In philosophy, though not in science, there are those who make such changes a matter of reproach. This, I think, results from the tradition which assimilates philosophy with theology rather than with science. For my part, I should regard an unchanging system of philosophical doctrines as proof of intellectual stagnation. A prudent man imbued with the scientific spirit will not claim that his present beliefs are wholly true, though he may console himself with

the thought that his earlier beliefs were perhaps not wholly false. Philosophical progress seems to me analogous to the gradually increasing clarity of outline of a mountain approached through mist, which is vaguely visible at first, but even at last remains in some degree indistinct.[1]

In this passage, Russell reproaches rigid adherence to beliefs and opinions and consequent refusal to change in the face of clear reason and evidence, as tends to happen in theology in contrast with science. He advocates for philosophy as well as for theology science's attitude to change. The point is that one who genuinely searches for the truth must be willing to change his/her views when compelling new knowledge and understanding become available. This is what the Law of Movement dictates.

The Law of Movement implies that we cannot achieve anything of significance without effort. Thus, indolence of whatever description (physical, mental, spiritual) offends against the Law of Movement, and therefore against the Will of God. And the different types of activities — spiritual, intellectual, and physical — must be kept in

---

[1] Robert E. Egner and Lester E. Denonn, editors. *The Basic Writings of Bertrand Russell* 1903-1959, New York, Simon and Schuster, 1967, p. 7

appropriate balance. Physical and intellectual efforts without spiritual activity are ultimately in vain.

It should be stated that there is a rhythm to the movement in Creation. We note that there is a rhythm to our breathing and to our heartbeat. Our activities must be similarly adjusted to a sensible rhythm; otherwise we harm ourselves. Workaholism (compulsive working without rest) and all frenzied activity go against the rhythm in Creation and are wrong.

By the same token, indolence and a complete retirement from work go against the Law of Movement. Research suggests several benefits from engaging in organized work even after retirement. In general, people who are inactive become unwell; retirees would benefit from the mental and spiritual engagement as well as the physical activity that comes with meaningful work.

Some studies show that the probability of suffering from clinical depression may increase by as much as 40 percent as a result of complete retirement from work. People who are active socially, physically, and intellectually are less likely to develop dementia, which is due to damage to the neurons in the brain. Dementia results in reduced or loss of intellectual capacity and personality integration. One major study reported that a sense of meaning and of purpose in life were associated with a longer lifespan. This is, of course, due to the fact that one cannot be idle if one sees some meaning and a definite purpose to one's life.

In accordance with the Law of Movement, no individual or group should rest on past glories. When we have attained a particular level or position of honour, we must strive to maintain it or else we would fall. It is only the spiritual sluggishness of humankind that permits people to enjoy reputations long after their activities have ceased to qualify them for such.

The Law of Movement commands us to live in the *present*, not in the past. Therefore, a person who is currently honourable should be treated as such, even if he had been a convicted criminal in the past. On the other hand, if a national hero becomes a criminal, he should be treated as a criminal. Persons who have been promoted to particular positions must continue to justify the higher appointments; they should be demoted to their new level of reduced competence should their performance decline.

The popular saying that "practice makes perfect", which associates improvement (though not necessarily perfection) with constant effort points to the Law of Movement. This Law, of course, applies in big as well as in small things. Some individuals, especially politically well-connected persons in some countries, have lost the ability and the discipline to do hard and honest work. This is because they have not done so for many years, having lived exclusively on political patronage and government largesse that were corruptly obtained. Society has a duty to create an environment in which such indolence and parasitism will become rare if not impossible.

Culture and traditional practices are also subject to the Law of Movement; they should be continually re-examined and, guided by the Laws of Creation, be adapted as necessary to changing times and circumstances.

Let us consider the expression "rest in peace", a popular prayer for the departed soul. It is a sign of widespread ignorance of and disregard for the Law of Movement that the vast majority of people of many cultures wish dead persons "everlasting rest." I suppose that some imagine that the activities of a life-time are enough for the entire existence. Perhaps, a major reason many people wish the soul to "rest in perfect peace" is that they consider work and earthly engagements as something of a curse and not the blessing that they are.

The reality, however, is that a departed soul cannot defy the Law of Movement; it cannot remain in everlasting rest. The wrong notion is one of the consequences of the pervasive lack of clarity about life after physical death. We should wish the physically dead "joyful activity", and not eternal rest. Just as a physical body in endless rest would soon die, so the soul in eternal repose would die; and in this case that would amount to spiritual death, eternal damnation.

Genuine happiness is achieved only through the active pursuit of earthly objectives that have high values and a spiritual content. But many human beings imagine that idleness makes for happiness. Indulgence, indolence, and base passions are unhealthy and can only lead to unhappiness and a wasted, purposeless life.

Enriching the Rich at the Expense of the Poor

For centuries, some statements in the Bible must have caused a great deal of concern to those who believe in the social philosophy advocating equality for all. Believers in this philosophy, called egalitarianism or equalitarianism, would be particularly irked by the idea of taking the little that the poor has and given it to the rich. Taken literally, that is what four closely similar verses in three different books of the New Testament imply. The statements bear directly on the matter of inequality and equity and are wrongly considered by many as taking a position on egalitarian or equalitarian philosophy. The passages are:

> **Mark 4:25**: "For to him who has will more be given; and from him who has not, even what he has will be taken away".

> **Matthew 13:12** and **Matthew 25:29**: "For to every one who has will more be given, and he will have abundance; but from him who has not, even what he has will be taken away".

> **Luke 19:26**: "I tell you, that to every one who has will more be given; but from

him who has not, even what he has will be taken away".

The verse in the Gospel according to Mark and that in Matthew 13:12 both came about in connection with the Parable of the Sower which Jesus had narrated to a large crowd. The Parable goes thus: As a sower went about planting, some seeds fell along the road and were eaten by birds. Some fell on rocky ground with little soil; they germinated but the seedlings soon withered and died for lack of moisture. Some seeds fell among thorns, they germinated but the thorns choked the growing plants, which in the end gave no yield. On the other hand, those seeds that fell into fertile soil had luxuriant growth and yielded seeds that were many multiples of the number of seeds planted.

When the disciples were alone with Jesus, they asked why Jesus spoke to the people in parables and also for the meaning of the Parable of the Sower. In answer to the first question, Matthew reports Jesus as saying: "*To you it has been given to know the secrets of the kingdom of heaven, but to them it has not been given. For to him who has will more be given, and he will have abundance; but from him who has not, even what he has will be taken away.* This is why I speak to them in parables, because seeing they do not see, and hearing they do not hear, nor do they understand" (Matthew 13:11-13, italics added).

The verses in Matthew 25:29 and in Luke are presented as the lesson of general applicability from two somewhat similar parables: the Parable of the Talents (Matthew 25: 14-30) and the Parable of the Pounds (also called "The Parable of the Gold Coins", Luke 19:11-27). Let me summarize the Parables. In the Parable of the Talents, a man going on a journey called his three servants and entrusted his property to them. To the first, he gave five talents, to the second, he gave two, and to the third, he gave one talent. A talent is an amount of money said to be equivalent to more than fifteen years' wages of a labourer in those days.

On his return, the servants individually accounted for what they had received. The one who got five talents had made an additional five and the second one had similarly made an additional two. But the third made excuses for not working with his one talent. He had simply buried it. The master ordered that the one talent be taken away from him and be given to the servant who already had ten talents. The master declared: *"For to every one who has will more be given, and he will have abundance; but from him who has not, even what he has will be taken away."*

Luke's Parable of the Pounds (the pound was worth three month's wages for a contemporary labourer) involved a nobleman and ten of his servants. The man before leaving for a far country to receive a kingdom called the servants and gave them one pound each and told them explicitly to trade with the amount until his return. When he came back, the nobleman called the servants to give an account of the gain they had made with the money. Luke reports only on three of the ten servants.

The first servant said that his one pound had generated ten more pounds. The nobleman commended him and gave him authority over ten cities. Another servant said he had made additional five pounds; he too was praised and given authority over five cities. But a third servant, who had not traded with his one pound but had simply kept it, returned it to the nobleman saying: "I was afraid of you, because you are a severe man; you take up what you did not lay down, and reap what you did not sow".

The nobleman chastised him, saying that the servant should have at least kept the money in the bank to earn interest. He asked that the one pound be taken away from the servant and given to the one who already had ten pounds. The nobleman then explained: "*I tell you, that to every one who has will more be given; but from him who has not, even what he has will be taken away.*"

The idea of taking away the little that a person has and giving it to one who already has much thus occurs in four separate passages in the New Testament. Since they are all attributed to the Lord Jesus Christ, directly or indirectly, the passages would be especially worrisome if interpreted literally as a guide for behaviour in our societies and in our relationships. That would mean a deliberate policy of enriching the richest at the expense of the poorest. Jesus Christ, as the incarnation of the Love of God, would certainly not advocate such a policy. *In these closely similar verses, Jesus was not setting out a policy; rather He was drawing attention to a Primordial Law and its consequence*: The Law of Movement.

As a consequence of the Law of Movement, talents that are used flourish and get even better; those that are not used degenerate and are finally lost. It is in this sense that we should understand and interpret the statement "*For to every one who has will more be given, and he will have abundance; but from him who has not, even what he has will be taken away*". In other words, a key lesson to be learned from the Parables of the Sower, the Talents, and the Pounds is that human beings must observe the Law of Movement and that there are bad consequences for those who do not conform to this immutable Primordial Law of Creation.

Human beings on earth do not have equal abilities and are not equally diligent in applying the abilities and the opportunities they have; therefore, they cannot be equal in their possessions and in their earthly circumstances. It is all a matter of perfect justice, brought about by the Law of Movement. The social philosophy of egalitarianism or equalitarianism does not accord with the Primordial Laws of Creation; it is wrong.

To avoid any misunderstanding, let me state right away that we human beings are all equal before the Primordial Laws. But this cannot translate into equality in the circumstances and conditions of all individuals because individuals do not obey the Laws to the same extent; their unequal extents of adjustment to the Laws result in unequal outcomes.

In accordance with the Primordial Laws, social, economic, and political systems should provide equal opportunities for all but should not seek to enforce equality of all. Some people make use of the opportunities offered but not to the same extent; others do not use the opportunities they are offered. Societies should, of course, also ensure that everybody is equal before the laws they make.

The Law of Movement also applies to the acquisition of spiritual knowledge. It is only those who seek seriously, constantly, genuinely and with humility, who will find the knowledge which leads to eternal life as well as happiness and success on earth, provided the knowledge is applied correctly. Those who indolently proclaim that the Truth cannot be known or that it is all superstition will, alas, never know the Truth.

The disciples of Jesus had, through their discipleship, demonstrated their serious and genuine search for Truth. Therefore, in accordance with the Law of Movement, they could expect, as Jesus told them, "to know the secrets (or mysteries) of the kingdom

THE LAW OF MOVEMENT   41

of heaven", secrets or mysteries which are denied to others who had not sought seriously enough or who sought in the wrong manner.

But anyone in the audience who heard the Parables told by Jesus and thereafter reflected deeply on their meanings (which would be tantamount to engaging in spiritual movement) would also be able "to know the secrets of the kingdom of heaven". Such people are the fertile soil on which the seeds fell, had luxuriant growth, and yielded seeds that were many multiples of the number of seeds planted. The Law of Movement implies that there should be no stand-still in one's search for truth; Christians who do so, for example, go against the teaching of Jesus!

In the realm of public policy, the Law of Movement implies that people should be rewarded according to their efforts; there should be equity. And governments should not attempt arbitrarily to make people equal regardless of their abilities and their efforts. And those who refuse to contribute to society, even though they could, do not deserve public support.

CHAPTER THREE

The Law of Attraction of Homogeneous Species

"Like always attracts like" is a Law of Creation. This Law is known as the Law of Attraction of Homogeneous Species and may also be called the Law of Attraction of Similar Species. The proverb "Birds of a feather flock together" hints at this Law. So also does the saying "Show me your friends and I will tell you who you are." Just as birds of a feather flock together, so do fishes of the same kind congregate and move together in large groups called schools. This grouping has many advantages for them. For example, fishes in schools find food more readily and are less prone to attack by predators. A fish that strays from its school exposes itself to the risk of being attacked and killed by enemy fishes and other predators.

Economists say that bad money drives out good money. This is like saying that unlike species repel, in accordance with the Law of Attraction of Homogeneous Species. Those who have studied chemistry might see the effect of this Law quite clearly in the coming together of identical molecules to form compounds, as well as in many chemical reactions. The Law manifests itself in the relationships among people, among animals, and even in the natural communities of plants.

The Law of Attraction of Homogeneous Species also ensures that if a particular species is split, the split parts will reunite when given an opportunity. It is for this reason that opposite poles of a magnet attract. The fact that unlike poles of a magnet attract appears, at first, to be a contradiction of the Law of the Attraction of Homogeneous Species. Let us, therefore, take some time to reflect on it.

Consider a bar magnet. Suppose we hold this magnet in such a way that the left end is the south pole and the right end is the north pole. Imagine that we then cut the bar magnet into two (the two parts need not be equal). We now have two bar magnets. Call the left piece "magnet A" and the right piece "magnet B". By convention, the right end of "magnet A is a new north pole, while the left end of "magnet B" becomes a new south pole. But remember that the right end of "magnet A" (the new north pole) and the left end of "magnet B" (the new south pole) were one and the same point before we cut the original bar magnet into two.

THE LAW OF ATTRACTION OF HOMOGENEOUS SPECIES 45

Therefore, when the new north pole attracts the new south pole, we are merely witnessing the coming together of closely similar parts that were forcibly separated; adjacent molecules that were separated are given a chance to reunite. And they do so, in accordance with the Creation Law of "Like Attracts Like". Whole species that are similar will attract. But so will the split parts of the same species seek to reunite.

Thus, the Law of Attraction of Homogeneous Species is fundamental for everything that is striving for union in Creation. But what appears to be attraction can be differentiated into *genuine attraction*, which takes place between *whole* species that are similar, and the *desire for union of split parts* of the same definite species.

The human being is not a whole species but only a splitting which carries within itself the desire for union. And this (sexual instinct apart) explains the attraction between man and woman. However, the thoughts, deeds, and volitions of human beings are whole species that attract homogeneous species. In general, a split species can give rise not only to split species but also to complete species.

It is through the mechanism of the Law of Attraction of Homogenous Species and the Law of Gravitation that hell came into being. *This is to say that hell is not the creation of God.* If people were not evil and did no evil, there would be no gathering of the evilminded; that is, there would be no hell. Contrary to the implications of the doctrines and teachings of some religions, there was no specific provision for hell in Creation and Subsequent Creation. God did not create hell.

Properly understood, hell is simply the flocking together of people who share similar weaknesses or evil characteristics. As evil people gather together, they inflict all sorts of evil on one another, thereby making life hell for every one of them. Hell has different sections according to different wrong dispositions – the greedy, the quarrelsome, the murderous, etc.

There are, of course, many gatherings of joy, peace, love, etc. formed under the pressure of the same Law of Attraction of Homogeneous Species. The beautiful and the hellish sections of the Beyond arose out of the volitions of human beings exercising their Free Will rightly or wrongly. We may also note that we encounter forms of hell right here on earth.

Stricter Separation in the Beyond

We have already stated that the effects of the Laws of Creation vary from species to species but that they are uniform within a given species. With human beings on earth, the physical body influences the effect of the Law of Attraction of Homogeneous Species in such a way that it is much less pronounced than it is in the Beyond where the physical body has been discarded. Thus, it is possible for a criminal to infiltrate the ranks of noble people on earth, for a period. In the Beyond the effects of the Law of Attraction of Homogeneous Species are so marked that the boundaries between all shades of good and bad people are very sharply drawn.

In the Beyond, criminals can only change through the suffering inflicted by fellow criminals; they cannot possibly interact with good persons and, therefore, cannot be positively influenced by them. On earth, however, criminals have the advantage that they can associate with noncriminal, upright citizens on account of the commonality of the physical body. Therefore, they can be directly counselled and influenced by good people, in addition to possible behavioural changes that may result from the earthly punishments to which caught criminals are subjected.

Similarly, persons with wrong religious or spiritual convictions have many painless opportunities on earth to realize their errors and, therefore, to change. However, in the Beyond they would find themselves only in the company of those who hold similarly wrong ideas; exchanges among them would amount to the blind leading the blind. Each one can come to recognition of his/her errors only through painful personal experiences.

On earth, the Law of Attraction of Homogeneous Species acting on the physical body makes it possible for persons of quite different inner character to interact, which rightly considered, is a great grace of the Creator. We should take advantage of the opportunities that such interactions offer and be thankful for the diversity that is thus made possible. We should for this reason place greater value on our time on earth. But we ought to be mindful of the company we keep.

Spiritual Qualities Come First

Because we are spiritual creatures, spiritual characteristics should be for us the most important factors of homogeneity. Perhaps as a way of teaching us this lesson, Jesus Christ, when told that His mother and His brethren were waiting to see Him, stretched forth His hand toward His disciples and said:

> Here are my mother and my brothers! For whoever does the Will of my Father in heaven, is my brother, and sister, and mother (Matthew 12:49-50, Revised Standard Version).

It is to be expected that superficial people and those who do not have any understanding for the inner and finer qualities of human beings would be attracted most readily only by outward appearances, such as skin colour, physical look, fashion, religious affiliation, etc. The fact that race and ethnicity are for many people the key considerations in their relationships with others and in their world-view is clear evidence of the pervasive superficiality and immaturity of humanity today.

With increasing spiritual knowledge, particularly the right knowledge of reincarnation, the relative unimportance of a person's race and nationality become obvious. This is because reincarnation, in the course of many earth-lives, may take a particular human spirit through different races, ethnic groups, and nationalities. Armed with that knowledge, it becomes easier for one to focus assessment of others on their worth as human beings: their personal characteristics, abilities, convictions, etc., all of which reflect individual levels of spiritual maturity.

Children and their Families

The Law of Attraction of Homogeneous Species and the Law of Reciprocal Action determine the family, place, and other circumstances into which one is born. Every thought, word or act gives rise to a "form" that has a characteristic consistency. Each "form" can be perceived with the sense appropriate to it. Thus, for example, thoughts can be "picked." This is not fantasy. In this connection, let us note that science has already shown that thoughts give rise to radiation that can be measured as well as forms of energy that can be applied in technologies, for example, to help paraplegics accomplish actions remotely.

An act of conception sends a form into creation alerting the human spirits in the Beyond of an opportunity for an incarnation on earth. Of the many souls in the Beyond that might wish or be compelled to incarnate, the one that does incarnate is determined by the spiritual environment of the parents,

THE LAW OF ATTRACTION OF HOMOGENEOUS SPECIES 51

particularly of the pregnant woman. Among possible specific factors would be the similarity between the volitions, strengths, weaknesses, propensities, etc. of the incoming soul and those of the prospective mother, father, or someone whom the mother allows to exert a strong influence on her around the time of incarnation. In addition to these, any threads of fate dating from past lives that link members of the family to the incoming soul, would also play a role.

Incarnation takes place about the middle of pregnancy. That is the time the incoming soul takes full possession of the foetus — the growing body, which it will use for its new earthlife. To ensure that nobody draws a wrong conclusion from this fact, we should state right away that it must not be imagined that abortion may be committed at any time without spiritual repercussion.

The act of procreation is like inviting the many anxious human spirits in the Beyond to get ready for a chance to experience an earthlife, with all the opportunities an earthlife offers for spiritual development. In the process, radiation threads are formed between the waiting soul and the foetus. Furthermore, the foetus takes shape according to a finer prototype, called the astral model. Termination of a pregnancy before incarnation thus, at least, amounts to frustrating and dashing the hopes of an aspiring soul, and destruction of the formed radiation threads as well as the developing astral model. In other words, the matter goes beyond the body of the pregnant woman. Therefore, abortion must have unpleasant consequences, regardless of earthly laws.

It is, of course, clear that abortion after incarnation has already taken place is, from the standpoint of the Laws of Creation, like physical murder. The solution is to avoid conception. We should never delude ourselves into believing that an action is necessarily without sin just because earthly laws permit it. We must always allow ourselves to be guided by the Will of God as expressed in His Laws and we should take into account knowledge of the mechanisms at work in the visible and invisible parts of Creation.

A noble spirit will, in general, incarnate in a family of noble people, by the Law of Attraction of Homogeneous Species, and, vice versa. Association with a not so honourable person by a pregnant woman may let down a bridge for the incarnation of a socalled black sheep. Nobility of spirit and, indeed, all spiritual characteristics (such as nobility of character, compassion, instinctive respect for justice, courage, etc.) are not biologically inherited. They occur among members of the same family through the operation of the Law of Attraction of Homogeneous Species.

Only physical, gross material characteristics are passed along through genetic processes. Nor are genetic processes by any means accidental. The Law of Reciprocal Action ensures that only those who have sown the necessary seeds are incarnated into families and places where they are bound to enjoy genetic advantage or suffer from hereditary handicap. For example, as a given disease is conquered in a particular part of the world, those whose karma call for that disease can only incarnate in another country where the disease has not been wiped out.

In reality, nobody is a victim of circumstance. It also follows that if we could rid the earth of all diseases and the causes of human suffering, any souls that need to experience suffering would be unable to incarnate on our earth. Similarly, if we would all strive to be noble in our thoughts, words, aspirations, deeds and intuitive perceptions, unworthy spirits would find it impossible to incarnate on earth. And thereby, the earth would eventually become like Paradise.

A Mirror into Our Inner Being

Through the Law of Attraction of Homogeneous Species, which ensures that like attracts like, the Omniscience of God has ensured that every human being is forced to carry openly for others to see a mirror in which his true self is quite clearly recognizable to the dispassionate and discerning observer. It is really not difficult to peep through the inner lives of people around us because what they think of other people they draw out of themselves, out of their own nature.

A really *good* human being will always only find the *good* in others and give expression to it. He will first consider everything according to *his* own nature, which is good. It is not a deliberate, willed process but an automatic one. The *good* person's inner goodness automatically attracts goodness in the person she comes across. Therefore, she instinctively sees and assumes goodness in the other person; unless, of course, there is no goodness to attract and to sense.

But an *evil* person is able to assume only *evil intentions* in other people, especially when it concerns matters which elude his understanding or are somewhat unclear to most people. His evil disposition radiates evil and automatically seeks out evil. An evil human being will interpret everything he does not yet understand as coming from the evil volition of another, because in accordance with his own nature, he simply does not expect anything else. As Abd-ru-shin (the author of the work *In the Light of Truth, The Grail Message*) puts it:

> An evil man can never believe in a good volition; he cannot believe that certain actions could spring from it, because he himself is incapable of it. He will dismiss selfless action as a myth, or even as a lie, because it is alien and incomprehensible to him. Only the *good man* can believe in it, because he himself is capable of acting likewise. Thus, a person's opinion of his fellow-men is always simply the *reflection of his own inner state*, which he clearly expresses in this way. Those who speak evil of their fellow-men, and spread it abroad, *must be evil in themselves*, or they would not do such things! (Lecture: "Distrust").

The fact that there is so much distrust and cynicism all around is proof of the abundance of evil human beings in the world. Those who regularly engage in and enjoy vile gossips often consider themselves better than those they gossip about. But the truth is that such people thereby unintentionally announce and publicize their own evil inner nature. "By their works you shall know them." Our works include what and how we speak!

Dispassionate but uncomplimentary comments can, of course, be made. But these can be easily recognized as they are usually sensitively expressed and invariably carry hints of understanding and love, whereas with gossips there is usually an undertone of superiority and arrogance. It is often the case that the most vociferous critics of public office holders do not necessarily perform better or even well when appointed to the positions of those they criticised. Their nature may be simply such that they are able to see only what is actually wrong or what they merely imagine to be wrong. By their criticisms they carry a mirror showing their own true nature.

The Speck in Our Neighbour's Eye

Jesus Christ alluded to a closely similar principle that expresses the Omniscience of God and the subtle working of the Law of Attraction of Homogeneous Species in the following admonition:

> Do not judge, so that you may not be judged. For with the judgment you make you will be judged, and the measure you give will be the measure you get. Why do you see the speck in your neighbour's eye, but do not notice the log in your own eye? Or how can you say to your neighbour 'Let me take the speck out of your eye,' while the log is in your own eye? You hypocrite, first take the log out of your own eye, and then you will see clearly to take the speck out of your neighbour's eye (Matthew 7: 1-5, New Revised Standard version).

The first two sentences are specifically about judging others. The correct judgment of individuals in any situation usually involves many factors that human beings are incapable of knowing and, therefore, cannot take into account. For example, the volition, motive, and the thought underlying any speech or action ought to be taken into account to make a fair judgment but invariably a third party cannot ascertain these. And, of course, our own nature and prejudices come into place in our assessments of even the factors that are observable. Thus, to avoid errors and sin, we should desist from judging.

The remaining verses, rightly understood, deal primarily with how we can infallibly know *our own* faults! Those verses are generally interpreted superficially as meaning that we should be lenient in considering the faults of other people. It is a good thing to be gracious and lenient when considering other people's faults but that is not the primary lesson of the cited admonition of Jesus.

In previous paragraphs, we stated that through what we instinctively say about and associate with other people we each hold a mirror into our own inner state. We noted that an evil person sees evil in others, even where such evil does not exist, whereas a good man readily sees what is good in another person. The good person tends not to notice any faults in another person unless and until he/she is shocked into realization of the other person's evil nature. Thus, we must have faults if we routinely and quickly see the faults of other people. Apart from leniency towards the faults of others, this should immediately suggest to us that we need to work hard on *ourselves*, if we care about self-improvement and if we wish to do the Will of God.

The primary objective of Jesus Christ with the admonition cited above is to make individuals mature spiritually by recognizing *their own* faults and striving to deal with those faults. Each individual is to use the faults of others that really disturb him as a measure of his own faults.

Let us consider how we go about it. If a person studies himself *objectively* he will soon realize that the faults which most disturb him in other people are very strongly rooted in himself and a cause of annoyance to his neighbours! Some people would simply shrug their shoulders or indicate only a mild and calm reaction when they notice a fault in another person, whereas some individuals would get agitated and visibly angry. The truth is that the agitated and angry persons are characterized by the observed fault to a much greater extent than the person in whom the fault was observed.

The expression of great annoyance and anger at the fault of another does not indicate moral high ground but rather the unintended announcement of the same but greater fault on the part of the disturbed person! When a person resorts to outbursts of rage because he has been lied to, do not be deceived into thinking that he is a truthful person. On the contrary, habitual liars are the ones most likely to react in that manner and they are also the ones who, even when dealing with obviously truthful persons, usually presume that those other people are lying.

CHAPTER FOUR
The Law of Reciprocal Action

Another Primordial Law of Creation is the Law of Reciprocal Action. It may be stated in the simplest of terms as "whatever we sow, we are obliged to reap". We know that if we sow maize, we can only reap maize, and if we want to harvest wheat, we must sow wheat. This Law ensures the maintenance of order and perfect justice in Creation. Imagine what confusion and bewilderment would result if we could not be certain what the harvest would be whenever we plant any seed; if at one time, a planting of maize gives us wheat, at another time the same planting gives us mango, etc.

Because of this Law, we know what harvest to expect with each planting, and what we must plant if we desire a particular harvest. Every effect has a cause; and every cause must result in an effect. Moreover, the Law of Reciprocal Action stipulates that the sower and no one else must reap what he/she sows.

It is important for us to note that this Law is no respecter of faith, belief, or religion. Indeed, this is true for all the Primordial Laws of Creation, since the Will of God does not depend on religion or human opinions. If a Christian sows maize, he will reap maize; so also will a Jew, a Muslim, a Buddhist, or a pagan. If a pagan sows goodness, he will reap goodness; so will a Bishop, a Hindu monk, or a Muslim Imam. In each case, it is the inner state of the individual and not the proclaimed faith that determines what is eventually reaped. Indeed, the Creator in His perfect Justice cannot be expected to be partial in the operation of His Laws.

This fact should lead us to the realization that religions and similar associations are only a means to an end, and not ends in themselves. If our religion helps us to understand thoroughly the true Will of the Almighty and shows us how to do this Will, then it has played its part. But we would be wrong to imagine that membership of any religion or sect would guarantee salvation. In the words of Abd-ru-shin, the Author of the Grail Message:

> On passing into the beyond every human being is divested of earthly power and its protection. Name, position, everything is left behind. Only a poor human soul passes over, there to receive and experience what it sowed. Not *a single* exception is possible! On

its path it is led through all the wheels of the relentless reciprocal action of Divine Justice. There is no church, no state, but only individual human souls who must personally account for every error they have made! (*In the Light of Truth, The Grail Message*, Volume I, Lecture: "Once Upon A Time ⋯!")

The Law of Reciprocal Action is hinted at in practically all scriptures and is considered valid in the doctrines of all religions, although it may be narrowly interpreted and poorly understood. For example, we find the following in the Bible: "vengeance is mine and recompense" (*Deuteronomy* 32:35). It is through the operation of the Law of Reciprocal Action that God metes out "vengeance" and "recompense" and not through personal intervention in the lives of individuals.

Contrary to the philosophy of deism, God is continually involved in Creation on matters of Creation-wide significance. However, God does not at all personally intervene to reward or punish individuals. His interventions are through the Primordial Laws of Creation and the activities of numerous invisible nonhuman beings that play various roles in upholding the Primordial Laws of Creation.

Free Will

One attribute of the human spirit that is particularly important in discussions of human beings in relation to the Primordial Laws of Creation, especially the Law of Reciprocal Action, is Free Will. Let us, therefore, digress a bit to discuss its origin and its significance.

Free Will is an inseparable part of the human spirit as distinct from the physical body (in which the intellect resides). When we think of a human being on earth, a picture that includes a head, two legs, two arms, etc. arises within us. Just as we do not picture a human being without a head, so there can be no human spirit without Free Will. A child's Free Will is dormant and only awakens fully in adulthood. While its Free Will is still dormant, the child has an active imitative instinct; it learns through imitation.

What does Free Will entail? It means simply that the human spirit is endowed with the ability to choose, to decide. It may choose to act or not to act, to do good or evil, to love or hate, to assist or hinder, to obey or break the law. Free Will lies in the freedom of decision and no more. The consequence of each decision rests exclusively on the immutable

Primordial Laws of Creation; laws that existed before the creation of the human spirit and against which it is powerless.

A man holding a loaded gun has the Free Will, the ability to decide whether or not to turn the gun on another person. If he does so, he is still free to decide whether or not to pull the trigger. Once he pulls the trigger, he has no control over what happens to his victim. It is always like that; we as human spirits are free to decide, but we are irrevocably subject to the consequences of every one of our decisions. And the rewards and punishments stipulated by earthly legal provisions do not substitute for the consequences of our choices as determined by the Primordial Laws of Creation.

In this connection, it is important to stress that whether or not a decision is made in a personal or official capacity, the decisionmaker will personally experience the consequence, in accordance with the Laws of Creation. Thus, all persons in authority, including judges, bear personal responsibility for the decisions they make and the actions they carry out while in office. This is one of the many reasons why we must strive for conviction in everything we do, so that we may gladly accept the consequences of all our decisions — whether they are made on behalf of a government, a corporation, a club or on our own behalf.

Earthly judges must be especially mindful of how they carry out the duties of their office. They must take true love as the basis, because it is only in true love that justice lies. And genuine love takes no account of what gratifies the other person and is agreeable to him/her. Rather, it considers only what will benefit the person *spiritually*.

Given that all the consequences of the exercise of our Free Will must fall upon us, we owe a duty to ourselves to be sure that we always make decisions which accord with the Will of God as expressed in the Primordial Laws of Creation. Whether we decide in ignorance or in full knowledge, the consequences will fall upon us. Therefore, we owe ourselves the duty to know the Laws of Creation. And we should never make decisions thoughtlessly or carelessly; we should always weigh matters carefully and with all the tools of our being, including our intellectual and spiritual faculties.

Some creatures, such as archangels and angels, do not have Free Will. They act strictly according to the Laws of Creation; thus, they never do wrong. Therefore, it is legitimate to ask why the human spirit is endowed with Free Will. The reason goes as follows: All that is spiritual by nature exercises the power of attraction in a manner analogous to magnets; the human spirit would attract indiscriminately if it did not have Free Will. Think of a hypothetical magnet that could attract indiscriminately — paper, iron, wood, soil particles, etc.; such a magnet would be useless for most practical purposes.

Similarly, the human spirit's ability to attract would overwhelm and incapacitate it, if it could not put a check on what it draws to itself and what it distances from itself. To prevent such possible incapacitation, the human spirit is given the ability to decide what to attract and what to reject. This is the origin of Free Will and it cannot be taken away from the human spirit. The gift or endowment of Free Will is also a demonstration of a principle that rests in Creation: the principle of balance. The inherent ability of the spirit to attract is balanced with the ability to choose what to attract. And by the same principle, the freedom to decide imposes the duty to take full responsibility for the decisions taken.

The human spirit, by exercising its Free Will and by being subjected to the consequences of its choices and decisions, acquires knowledge through experience, and thus matures. As it matures, it is increasingly able to make only those decisions that advance the spiritual goal of its existence on earth. And at full maturity, back home in Paradise, it is, like the angels, able to make only decisions that accord with the Will of the Creator.

It is not accidental that human beings generally desire freedom to choose. Political, social and economic systems should make this possible. And, of course, freedom of religion and of thought should be guaranteed. However, as implied above, societies must also ensure that individuals are held accountable for the choices they make through appropriate legislation and policies. By so doing, the *quality* of the exercise of Free Will is enhanced. Many moral evils in the world are due to denial of people's freedom to decide as well as failure to hold people accountable for the decisions they make.

The Law of Reciprocal Action, which operates throughout Creation, is God's mechanism for influencing the human spirit's use of its Free Will. This Law ensures that we reap multiples of whatever we sow in thought, word, or deed. If the harvest gives joy, one is encouraged to sow more of similar seeds; a harvest of painful experiences dissuades one from sowing more of the same. All the policies of societies should aim at complementing this God-willed process. Since the harvest always indicates the sowing, bad and painful experiences must be seen as reminders of some past wrong-doing and, therefore, the imperative to change for the better. We do not need to remember specifically what we did wrong or when.

By choice, we inflict evil on fellow human beings. And in accordance with the Law of Reciprocal Action we have to reap multiples of the evil consequences at the appropriate later time, which means yet more evil.

Similarly, societies and their governments make bad policy choices and sometimes refuse to adopt obviously sensible policies. The consequences are again multiple evils. For example, many governments have refused to take necessary measures to preserve the environment and they are doing nothing about climate change because of short-term economic considerations. Such economic myopia must in future lead to natural disasters. And then people, including those who failed to act, would thoughtlessly ask, "Why does God allow natural disasters?"

Free Will ensures that we are able to decide what we will sow in thought, word, or deed. Having taken the decision, the Law of Reciprocal Action in cooperation with the other Primordial Laws takes over. *We are to leave vengeance to God's Law of Reciprocal Action not out of kindness or consideration for those who may offend us but for our own sake.* In trying to retaliate, we might do something bad and thereby sow a bad seed that would result in more harm to us in future. Whenever we retaliate we open a new cycle of wrong-doing that may harm not only the original offender but ourselves as well, in accordance with the Law of Reciprocal Action.

"Vengeance" and "recompense" are nothing but the reciprocal effect of a man's evil or good deeds, which takes place strictly and justly according to the Laws of Creation, "eye for eye, tooth for tooth, hand for hand, foot for foot" (Deuteronomy 19:21). The expressions "eye for eye, tooth for tooth" etc. mean that the reciprocal effects are of the same kind as the original cause. Seed and harvest are of the same kind; hence suffering for suffering, and joy for joy. Just as rice grows only from the grain of rice so does an evil volition always gives rise to evil and a good volition can give rise only to good.

Therefore, these Biblical words are not to be taken in the earthly sense but in the spiritual sense. Human beings must leave "vengeance" and "recompense" to the Primordial Laws of Creation. They must not engage in personal revenge by, for example, knocking out the evil-doer's teeth or plucking his eyes when the latter has done the same to them. For it is explicitly stated: "Vengeance is mine, I will repay!" And the appropriate "vengeance" and "repayment" are more just than human beings could possibly imagine.

More on the Law

Let us learn a bit more about this Law, which holds the key to so many unsolved problems. We must, of course, understand that "sowing" is not limited to its ordinary agricultural sense. We "sow" through our thoughts, our words, our volitions, as well as our actions. This implies that we are all constantly sowing, be it only in our thinking and in our general attitude to life. If our thoughts are always good, we reap harvests of blessings; if they are evil, then we heap evils on ourselves. As we shift gear between good and evil, so do the harvests change.

We know that quite often people's actions are different from their thinking and their volition.

A man may be smiling at you and saying nice words to you while planning to harm you; his volition is in conflict with his words and actions. A man makes a donation to an organization even though he does not share the ideals and the objectives of the organization He simply wants the publicity or seeks favour from members of the organization. In all such cases, the Law of Reciprocal Action ensures that the harvests are weighed carefully to reflect not only the actions, but also the ulterior motives.

Most human beings cannot read other people's thoughts nor fathom their real volitions. And so, they cannot be good judges in the sense of the Primordial Laws of Creation. Hence we must not make ourselves judges over other people, because most of us lack the ability to judge correctly. For even when we observe the action and hear the words, we may not know the motives.

Another aspect of the Law of Reciprocal Action, which we must note, is that one planted seed yields, at harvest, many seeds. The harvest is of the same kind (quality or species) as what was sown but its quantity is much greater. Thus our actions, good or bad, return to us multiplied. The increase is the result of another Primordial Law — the

Law of Attraction of Homogeneous Species that has already been discussed.

Interval between Sowing and Reaping

Moreover, we should note that the interval between sowing and reaping depends on what is sown. Some grain crops are ready for harvest four months after planting, whereas some tree crops do not yield any harvests until after many years. Indeed, we plant some trees knowing full well that they will not be ready for harvesting in our lifetime.

Even for the same crop, the period required for maturity may vary according to variety. For example, traditional varieties of cowpeas, also called beans, a food legume that is highly relished in West Africa, northeast Brazil, and southern United States, mature in about 100 days. Modern varieties of the same crop are ready for harvesting in about 60 days after planting.

Such differences in periods to maturity also apply to the actions, thoughts, words, prayers, and volitions of people. The necessary interval between sowing and reaping is the key to the riddle of why good things may be happening to an apparently bad person and why bad things may be happening to an apparently good person. The good that may currently be falling on the laps of a seemingly bad person must be the good he did in the past. Conversely, the bad experiences of the person who is presently striving to do only what is good are the consequences of some wrong done in the past, which are only now ready for harvest.

And we should always remember that we are usually not qualified to judge who is good or bad. As previously stated, this is because we are incapable of knowing people's thinking, motivations, and volitions even, when we hear their words and observe their actions. The perfect Justice of God does not permit any arbitrariness. One reaps only what one has personally sown, and nobody reaps what he or she has not sown.

In our vanity, often veiled, we are sure we deserve the good things that come our way but feel unfairly treated when bad things happen to us. There appear to be injustices in some cases only because of our own ignorance. A key aspect of this ignorance is lack of the knowledge of reincarnation or its deliberate rejection. The truth is that some "fruits" we now harvest, whether they are good or bad, were planted in some distant past, in previous earth-lives. On the other hand, some "seeds" we are now sowing may not be ready for harvest until a distant future, in the Beyond, or in another earth-life.

Readers who desire detailed information on the subject of reincarnation may wish to consult Stephen Lampe's *The Christian and Reincarnation*[1].

The Creator grants every human being the Free Will to decide what he/she may or may not sow; but once one has done the sowing, one is obliged irrevocably to "eat the harvest". It does not matter who the person is.

Many persons readily associate the Law of Reciprocal Action with Divine Justice. But relatively few realize that in this Law also lies Divine Love. Consider a person who sows a good seed. The Law guarantees that at harvest he receives fruits of the same kind, and this can be perceived as Justice. However, the effect of the Law is not only on quality or kind, but also on quantity. A person who sows, for example, one seed of maize, may reap two cobs of maize containing hundreds of seeds. Is it not Love, when for one good seed, the Law of Reciprocal Action ensures a return of hundreds of good seeds?

---

[1] Stephen M. Lampe, *The Christian and Reincarnation*, Legacy Edition. Ibadan, Millennium Press, 2008. x, 257p.

Let us also note that Divine Love considers only what is of benefit to us spiritually. And what carries spiritual benefits may sometimes be quite uncomfortable or painful to us. Indeed, we must redefine love in our relationships with fellow human beings in terms of what will benefit them spiritually. In this connection, it may be remarked that some human actions and attitudes as well as ideologies that appear to demonstrate love are unhelpful and wrong when viewed from a spiritual perspective.

The bitter fruits of the bad seeds we sowed are spiritually helpful reminders of the fact that we strayed from the way ordained by the Creator. Any adversity, pain or suffering should be seen as cues, hints of the need to reexamine our understanding of the Laws of the Creator and how we stand in relation to them. Such reexaminations, if done in genuine humility, are bound to help us to grow spiritually, and achieve happiness here on earth. As we learn the right lessons and make necessary adjustments so that we sow only good seeds, the Law of Reciprocal Action assures us of bountiful harvests of good fruits, at the appropriate times. And this, surely, is Love.

Therefore, we see that the Law of Reciprocal Action is a way by which God shows His Love, while at the same time ensuring His Justice. For Divine Justice and Divine Love cannot be separated; they are one! God does not inflict suffering and tragedy on people. People bring them about purely by themselves, and by a process through which they could also ensure abundance, happiness, and bliss for themselves.

Attitude to the Suffering

Let us, right away, raise and answer a question of great social importance that may well arise at this point in the minds of wellmeaning people: does it follow from all these that we do not have to worry about suffering people since they are themselves responsible for their suffering? That is, may we maintain that they are only reaping what they sowed in this earthlife or in an earlier one and do not therefore deserve our help? *The Law of Reciprocal Action should suggest the opposite to us*. The Law shows clearly the need to do good at all times; for whatever good we do and to whomever we do it, be it an evil or good person, we stand to reap the good fruits.

In reality, any good we do, we do for ourselves; since the fruits return to us as multiples of the seeds of our benefaction. Whenever we see somebody suffering, we should consider ourselves as having an opportunity to sow good seeds. We should not concern ourselves with the cause of the person's suffering; we should not judge.

Moreover, we should know that, in the perfection of the Laws of the Creator, if a sufferer does not deserve help, nobody who is in a position to help will come into contact with him or her. And how do we know that our relationships in former earthlives are not such that we owe the particular suffering person a debt that we must pay through offering help at that point? Let it be stressed, however, that true help is always only that which takes cognizance of and facilitates the recipient's spiritual advancement.

Mission Karma

Furthermore, we should note that not all suffering is a consequence of a past evil. A person's suffering may be due to "mission karma". Mission Karma is a fate, a consequence, a sacrifice that a person voluntarily accepts in order to fulfil a particular mission. Suppose a house is burning and I enter it to save a child trapped in it. By undertaking the mission, I accept voluntarily the possibility, indeed the likelihood, of having some burns; any burns or harm I suffer are the karma associated with my mission of mercy.

The idea of mission karma helps to deepen further our understanding of the working of the Law of Reciprocal Action. Mission karma explains, for example, how it was possible for Jesus Christ to be murdered even though He obviously and definitely was sinless. That is, the murder was not the fruit of His sowing.

Even before Jesus set out on His mission of salvation, it was appreciated that Darkness had descended heavily on earth, that men had become exceedingly evil and confused, that even their religious leaders sought only earthly power and influence and were no longer interested in the truth. It was, therefore, clear that earthmen *could* reject His teachings and *might* even kill Him. Because Jesus was, and is the personification of Love, He accepted the risk, in the manner that a man, who out of love, dashes into a burning house to save a trapped child accepts the risk of burns.

It should, of course, be easy to understand that the man who voluntarily, and out of genuine love, accepts a mission that is associated with dangers is at the same time sowing good seeds, seeds of pure love. The seeds will grow, mature and, in due course, yield a bountiful harvest. Such harvests arising from acts of selfless love are the treasures we store for ourselves in heaven; they form points of anchor for the invisible threads that could pull us to Paradise.

CHAPTER FIVE

The Law of Reciprocal Action and the Matter of Forgiveness

In explaining the Law of Reciprocal Action, it was stated that one reaps whatever one sows without fail. This being so, one might ask if forgiveness is possible within the framework of the Primordial Laws of Creation. The short answer would be yes, of course! The Will of God does allow for forgiveness; for God is not only Justice, He is also Love. Divine Justice and Divine Love are inseparable. That both Justice and Love are built into the Law of Reciprocal Action has already been noted and illustrated.

The Spiritual Meaning of Forgiveness

As a starting point, let us examine the spiritual meaning of forgiveness. It is the complete wiping away of a wrongdoing in such a manner that it is as if the forgiven person never committed that particular wrong. It is this meaning that is implied in a statement in the Book of Isaiah, three versions of which are reproduced below:

> I, I am He who blots out your transgressions for my own sake, and I will not remember your sins (*Isaiah* 43:25, Revised Standard Version).

> I, I it is who blots out your acts of revolt for my own sake and shall not call your sins to mind (Isaiah 43:25, New Jerusalem Bible).

> I, even I, am He who blots out your transgressions for my own sake; And I will not remember your sins (Isaiah 43:25, New King James Version).

It should be easy to understand that forgiveness in this sense of complete wiping away of a wrongdoing, of "blotting out" of guilt, cannot come to a person of evil disposition. It can only be granted to those who have resolved firmly and earnestly to do the Will of God; those who are determined to keep their thoughts pure and, who as a matter of course, desist from doing anything that would harm their neighbours.

To understand the natural process that leads to forgiveness, we start with the knowledge that everything takes on form; our thoughts, words, actions and every movement of our spirit give rise to forms. The nature of the form and the plane of existence to which it belongs depend on its origin. Thus, forms arising from thoughts differ from those of words, which are in turn different from those of actions etc. A man's weaknesses and propensities from which arise his wrong and evil thoughts, words, and deeds also have forms that take root in him.

As we think, speak or act, appropriate forms that take root in us are sent into Creation. These forms attract or are attracted by their own types, in accordance with the Law of Attraction of Homogeneous Species. At the right time, such forms return to us multiplied and we are obliged to harvest the fruits corresponding to the nature of the original thoughts, words, or deeds. It should be stated again that this reciprocal action, this harvesting of what one has sown, is not a punishment; *God does not punish.* Bitter experiences are opportunities and helps for one to recognize how one stands in relation to the Will of God.

As we reap the returning bitter fruit, the form that arose from us is uprooted, and the particular guilt is redeemed, provided that we consciously recognize that we deserve the bitter fruit and commit ourselves to change; as happened with the Biblical Penitent Thief on the Cross.

It is sadly the case that often, while we are suffering as a consequence of an earlier wrongdoing, we question and doubt the Justice of God. One often hears people asking: "Why must this happen to me?" Many react angrily, curse and swear, when confronted with the bitter fruits of their own sowing. Through such reactions, they perpetuate cycles of sowing evil and reaping evil for themselves.

On the other hand, an earnest resolution for what is good, and a firm conviction in the Justice and Love of the Almighty ensure that the soil for conscious wrongdoing and evil ceases to exist in one. One's weaknesses and propensities wither away, and one may then expect forgiveness. On this matter, the author of The Grail Message declares:

> Reformation alone is the living road to forgiveness! (*In the Light of Truth, The Grail Message*, Volume II, Lecture: "I Am the Lord Thy God").

And the forgiveness earned in this manner is so complete that it is as though no offence was ever committed. In the Parable of the Prodigal Son, we recall that once the son penitently found his way back to his father, he was treated as though he had never gone astray.

Forgiveness is Not Arbitrary

Many religious people assume that forgiveness is arbitrary; that one can obtain it by simply asking. This is not the case. The Creator in His perfection never acts arbitrarily in anything. The Grace of the Almighty does exist, but only those who have fulfilled the conditions prescribed by the Primordial Laws of Creation can enjoy it. Those who go against or ignore the Primordial Laws are automatically barred from God's Grace.

Our Lord, Jesus Christ said that He did not come to destroy the Law, which includes the Law of Reciprocal Action. And so in the prayer that He gave to mankind, we find this statement: "And forgive us our trespasses, as we forgive those that trespass against us." And on another occasion, Jesus Christ told His disciples:

> And whenever you stand praying, forgive, if you have anything against anyone; so that your Father also who is in heaven may forgive you your trespasses. But if you do not forgive, neither will your Father who is in heaven forgive your trespasses (Mark 11: 25-26, Revised Standard Version).

These are clear declarations that forgiveness is not unconditional, not arbitrary. If we want forgiveness, we must work for it. It is also a statement of the Law of Reciprocal Action — to "reap" forgiveness, one must "sow" forgiveness. In addition to achieving forgiveness through suffering the full consequence of a wrongdoing, there is another process by which one may earn forgiveness. It is through what might be called symbolic redemption, a process that accords fully with the Primordial Laws.

Symbolic Redemption

To illustrate the process of symbolic redemption, let us recall our statement that everything takes on form. A person who is firmly resolved to give purity to his/her every thought, word, and deed is enveloped by good forms. These forms attract their own kinds and they become a strong, possibly impenetrable protective shield around him/her. Any evil forms, arising from past thoughts, words or actions, that may approach are deflected and repulsed by the layer of good forms now surrounding him/her, since unlike forms must repel. Thus, such a person would not experience the consequences of the earlier wrongdoing.

The strength of the invisible protective layer depends on the strength of the person's goodness. It can happen that the incoming evil forms are able to penetrate the protective layer; but even then they would be weakened. As an illustration, a guilt which would otherwise have imposed a prison term on a man could be redeemed through his simple act of lovingly helping a child or an elderly person to cross a busy street. The help so rendered, purely out of love, becomes the act that redeems his past grievous guilt. He has earned symbolic redemption.

Thus, we note that symbolic redemption is anchored on the Primordial Laws. It is not arbitrary. Suppose we think, speak or do an evil. The appropriate evil form goes forth into Creation and gathers strength by attracting existing forms similar to it. Eventually, it returns to us as multiples of its original self. However, the impact, the effect it would have on us, depends on how we stand spiritually at the time of its return. If we are still our old evil selves, we would attract the incoming evil consequence in accordance with the Law of Homogeneous Species. The incoming evil would, therefore, hit us with full force, unleashing its full impact on us.

However, if before the evil consequence returns, we have changed and become good, we would automatically repel it; again in compliance with the same Law of Attraction of Homogeneous Species. How effectively we repel, or force back the returning bad fruit of our evil thought, word, or deed, would depend on how much we have changed for the better.

If we have changed sufficiently, the returning bad fruit would be shattered and it would have no unpleasant effect on us, or the effect might be so slight that we would hardly notice it. For such slight harm, the Yoruba people of Nigeria have an apt saying: that one should be grateful in that what could have cut one's head, has merely removed one's cap! This is forgiveness — symbolic redemption.

Conversely, one might not harvest the joys one had sown in the past, if one has become evil at the time the good fruits return. Also, the help sent to us in answer to a prayer may not reach us because of our own evil heart. Thus, we see in all simplicity that we are, indeed, the architects of our own fates, and that forgiveness depends on us and is always within our reach.

We can obtain "forgiveness" the hard way through experiencing the full consequences of our volitions, thoughts, words, or deeds; or through the easy way by becoming good. "Good" not as defined by us or by our flatterers but as determined by the extent to which we live according to the Will of the Almighty, according to how we obey the Primordial Laws of Creation. Obviously, we can only do God's Will, if we understand It. Therefore, our first task is to become thoroughly familiar with the Primordial Laws that manifest the Will of God in Creation.

Who Can Forgive?

We have emphasized the teaching of Jesus Christ that we should forgive those that offend us. This teaching implies that everybody has the power to forgive any offences committed against him or her; if we did not have the power to forgive, Jesus would not require us to forgive. He would never ask us to do what we could not do. And the fact that in all His teachings and actions, Jesus always upheld the Will of God must be emphasized. Thus, His teaching that we should forgive, accords fully with the Primordial Laws of Creation.

Let me outline how it is that we are able to forgive the sins committed against us. I explained earlier that with our every action, word or thought, an invisible form (a thread of fate) arises and takes root in us. This form goes forth, attracted by other forms that arose from similar actions, words or thoughts thereby the form becomes much stronger. In due course, the strengthened form returns to us fully laden with the appropriate harvest.

When we commit a sin, the victim of the sin is linked by invisible threads to the form that arises. Because of this connection, the victim has the power to cut the threads of fate arising from the sin. Through his heartfelt decision not to avenge or take offence and his desire that the offender should not suffer for the sin, the victim cuts the threads. Because the threads are cut, the form withers; the offender is thereby set free from the consequences of that particular sin.

Therefore, an important way by which we can earn forgiveness is to plead for forgiveness with the victims of our offences We should go directly to the person we offended, acknowledge or "confess" our wrongdoing and plead for forgiveness. In this connection, it is important to note that whereas the person offended can forgive, a third party, who is in no way affected, does not have the power to forgive. A third party, such as a clergyman, is not in any way linked with the form that arose as a result of the offence and, therefore, he does not have the power to cut the threads of fate involved. This is why a clergyman cannot forgive the sins of anybody, except the sins committed against him *personally.*

The presumption that a priest can forgive the sins of members of his church is probably based on what Jesus is reported to have told His Disciples immediately after His resurrection:

> If you forgive the sins of any, they are forgiven; if you retain the sins of any, they are retained (*John* 20:23, Revised Standard Version).

Jesus is reported to have made the statement when He suddenly appeared to ten of his Disciples (Judas Iscariot had committed suicide, and Thomas was not present) who were assembled in a locked room. He blessed them and sent them forth to spread His Message, and then told them that whichever sins they forgave would be forgiven, and those they did not forgive would not be forgiven.

The right understanding of what Jesus told His disciples is simply that they had the power to forgive or not to forgive any sins committed against them personally, as individuals. Jesus was definitely not giving them a general license to forgive sins perpetrated against other people. In accordance with the Laws of His Father, which Jesus knew and upheld at all times, the Disciples could not forgive the sins of third parties.

If we recall the intolerable sufferings to which the Disciples were later subjected, the grievous sins perpetrated against them as they spread the teachings of Jesus Christ, we would readily understand why their Master needed to remind them that they had the power to forgive or not to forgive their torturers and murderers. Jesus was, in effect, urging His Disciples to forgive the sins that He knew would be committed against them in the course of spreading His Message.

Forgiveness, like everything else, is governed by the Laws that God put into Creation from its very beginning. Therefore, arbitrary forgiveness of sin is impossible. It is for this reason that a third party, that is, somebody who is not in any way connected with an offence cannot grant forgiveness for that offence. If I offend Mr. Doe, I should seek forgiveness from Mr. Doe, not from a priest. A priest may counsel or advise me, but he does not have the power to forgive me, no matter what he or anybody else may believe. A priest can, of course, forgive whatever sins anybody commits against him *personally*, just like everybody else.

The Sin Against the Holy Spirit

We have indicated in the foregoing sections that a sin may be forgiven directly by the victim of the sin. It may also be forgiven symbolically through a complete inner change on the part of the sinner before the fruits of the sin return to him. A third way by which a sin is "forgiven" is through suffering the full consequences of the sin. This process, which involves the full experiencing of the consequences of one's wrongdoing according to the Law of Reciprocal Action, is not considered as forgiveness by most people. Forgiveness is assumed not to entail reaping of any bitter fruits, or suffering any bad consequences for an offence. In this sense one obtains forgiveness only by being forgiven by the offended person or through obtaining symbolic redemption in the manner already described.

Once one has harvested what one sowed, a cycle is completed and it is as if one had never committed that particular sin. But the sinner may start another cycle of sowing and reaping depending on his reaction to the harvest. If he does not acknowledge any wrong-doing but, for example, blames others for his problems, the root of the sin remains and he thereby sows a new bad seed.

An understanding of these processes by which forgiveness is granted or earned holds the key to a Biblical statement that must have baffled many students of the Bible. It is the statement that implies that any sin may be forgiven, but not the sin or blasphemy against the Holy Spirit (Matthew 12: 3132; Mark 3:29, and Luke 12:10). Many people must wonder why it is that blasphemy against the Holy Spirit cannot be forgiven, even though a sin against the Son of God can be forgiven.

Jesus personifies the Love of the Almighty, whereas the Holy Spirit is the Executive Will of God who is responsible for the World Judgment. The Work of the Holy Spirit lies in the unchanging and incorruptible Primordial Laws of Creation. Jesus Christ did forgive sins committed against Him; for example, on the crucifixion cross, He said "Father, forgive them, for they know not what they do." It is clear, therefore, that sins committed against Jesus, the Love of God, can be forgiven.

On the other hand, the Holy Spirit is the Justice of the Almighty Who works through and personifies the immutable Primordial Laws. Any sin against the Holy Spirit brings about unfailingly the full consequence dictated by the Law of Reciprocal Action. In short, whereas a sin against Jesus Christ could be forgiven by Jesus Himself, that against the Holy Spirit compels the sinner to go through the mills of the Law of Reciprocal Action. The one who sowed the seed must reap it; no one else can reap it for him.

We certainly can say that we have it on the authority of Jesus Himself that anybody who sins against the Holy Spirit will not be forgiven and, therefore, Jesus could not have died for such sins. Remember what Jesus said:

> Think not that I have come to abolish the law and the prophets; I have come not to abolish them but to fulfil them (Matthew 5: 17).

Nobody can forgive any sins against the Holy Spirit. For this reason, Jesus could not have reaped the fruits resulting from the sins that others had committed or may commit against the Holy Spirit. Therefore, the murder of Jesus on the cross could not have taken away such sins.

The Attitude of the Victim

The discussion so far has centred on how the offender obtains forgiveness. Let us now consider forgiveness from the standpoint of the victim of the offence. We have, in fact, already done so indirectly. We did so when we quoted the admonition contained in the Lord's Prayer that we should forgive those that offend us so that our Heavenly Father may forgive us our own sins. The same admonition is made in the Bible passage in Mark (11:25-26) quoted earlier.

Thus, the position of the victim of an offence is clear: he is provided an opportunity to sow forgiveness so that he may reap forgiveness. If he does not take advantage of the opportunity, he is the loser for it. Our decision to forgive should, therefore, not depend on the attitude of the offender. We should forgive, whether or not the offender is repentant. In accordance with the Primordial

Laws of Creation, whenever we forgive, we are bound to reap forgiveness, regardless of the condition or attitude of the person who wronged us.

When offended, we sometimes consider it necessary to react, and after reacting we may find ourselves wondering if we have not burdened ourselves with guilt. It should be understood that some of our reactions that may be unpleasant to the offender may not *necessarily* be wrong.

Consider that the Son of God drove out those who were selling and buying in the temple and "overturned the tables of the moneychangers and the seats of those who sold pigeons" (Mark 11:15). It was in the best interest of the sellers, buyers, and moneychangers to be forcibly prevented from continuing to desecrate or defile the temple. Thus, the action of Jesus was borne out of genuine love. We know that parents must sometimes deal severely with their own children not because they hate them but, on the contrary, out of love.

Therefore, we may take action against offenders but we must be certain that our reactions are well-considered and definitely not ill-motivated. We should never act out of vengeance but out of love for the offender. In this connection, we should also understand that genuine love considers only that which is of *spiritual* benefit to the person loved. In reacting, most people unfortunately allow their own weaknesses to take sway; they react in retaliation and with no thought whatsoever of what would truly change the offender. Before we react, we must reflect very carefully, lest we burden ourselves with guilt.

Forgiveness and Reincarnation

Let us recall the link between forgiveness and reincarnation. Some of the offences or sins we commit are not forgiven before we die. The nature of many such offences is such that the consequences must be experienced on earth. And so we are obliged to return to the earth 'to harvest our plantings.'

Some repent only on their deathbeds, out of fear, uncertainty, simple prudence or because of better spiritual understanding as the connection between the physical body and the soul begins to loosen. This lastminute change of heart happens so frequently that a term has been coined for it — the deathbed repentance syndrome. It should be easy to understand that, according to the Divine

Laws, such repentance will bring help in the Beyond and in a subsequent earthlife only to the extent that it represents genuine and permanent spiritual change.

But many who die suddenly do not even have time to consider change. And others are too confused or debased to think about a spiritual change. Consider, for example, the man who kills many people and then commits suicide. For these and other reasons, many human spirits carry huge loads of sins with them into the Beyond.

The inexplicable blows of fate and the diverse uncomfortable circumstances that we observe everywhere on earth are the consequences of the unsettled old debts that men carry over from previous earthlives, and any fresh debts they incur during current earthlives. God is absolutely just. But only an understanding of His perfect and unchanging Laws as well as the reality of reincarnation can lift the fact of God's absolute Justice from mere belief to strong conviction.

CHAPTER SIX

The Law of Gravitation

Another Primordial Law of Creation is the Law of Gravitation. The Law, which may also be called the Law of Spiritual Gravity, operates throughout Creation. It may be explained by reference to the physical law of gravity, which is the form in which this Law manifests on earth. Whatever is really light rises easily, whereas that which is heavy tends to fall.

This is how Herbert Vollmann illustrates the Law of Gravitation: "When, for example, we put a piece of iron and a piece of cork in water, the iron sinks immediately owing to its heaviness but the cork remains on the surface. If we press the cork to the bottom of the water and let go, it rises. The process in the world invisible to us is exactly the same when, for instance, man has laid aside his physical body. If we have made it heavy through base propensities, the ethereal body which is separated from the physical body sinks to that place in the Beyond which is of the same heaviness····. Or if through striving for higher and purer things we have made it lighter, the ethereal body floats upwards like a cork into more luminous realms."[1]

---
[1] Herbert Vollmann, *A Gate Opens*, Stuttgart, Stiftung Gralsbotschaft Publishing Co., 1995. Composite Volume, p. 25

A human being has not only the physical body but several other nonphysical bodies. At death, the spirit drops its physical cloak; that is, it leaves its physical body behind. Where the spirit, with its nonphysical cloaks (the soul), finds itself is then determined by the Law of Gravitation. The Law of Gravitation is the automatic mechanism by which the human spirit ascends to Paradise as it matures or descends to the realms of darkness and damnation as it chooses to engage in what is evil.

Thoughts, Words, and Actions Can Lift or Sink

Evil doing, bad thoughts, wrong aspirations and attitudes make the spirit heavy. Such heaviness causes it to sink, to fall away in a direction opposite from that of its origin. That is, it retrogresses. How deep it sinks, depends on how much it has immersed itself in wrongdoing, and therefore how heavy it has become. Following its fall, it congregates with other spirits that have similar weaknesses; this is, again, in accordance with the Law of Attraction of Homogeneous Species.

If, for example, greed is one of its major vices, it would get drawn to others who are as greedy and these would inflict greed on him continuously. The gathering of the greedy, constantly perpetrating greed on one another thereby forms a "greed section" of hell. Any member, who, through the distasteful experience in this section, becomes disgusted with greed and no longer wishes to be a part of it, is automatically moved away. For, through its disapproval of the place, its ethereal body would have become less heavy than that of the environment; and the Law of Gravitation as well as the Law of Attraction of Homogeneous Species would ensure its separation to an environment more appropriate to its new state.

Noble actions, thoughts, and attitudes make the spirit light; so that, once it has shed the physical body, it rises automatically toward its spiritual origin, its home. It rises along with similarly noble spirits from which it receives love, and to which it also gives love.

Tempting Jesus to Defy Gravity

That nobody can go against this Law (or any Primordial Laws of Creation) is alluded to in the story of the devil's temptation of Jesus in the desert. The devil wished to harm the mission of Jesus right at the very beginning by making Jesus attempt to do what is not in accordance with the Will of God. Therefore, it urged Jesus to jump down from the pinnacle (or parapet) of the Temple in Jerusalem to prove that He was the Son of God.

Jesus, of course, knew that the Law of Gravitation could not be annulled for His own sake or for the sake of anybody; thus, He did not fall for the temptation. If Jesus had thrown Himself down from the pinnacle of the Temple, He would have been very badly hurt, in accordance with the Law of Gravitation. And that would have been an embarrassing spectacle and a major setback to His mission.

Thomas Aquinas on Spiritual Gravity

Thomas Aquinas, recognized by the Roman Catholic Church as its foremost philosopher and theologian, describes how departed souls reach their "places", their immediate destinations. In his *Summa Theologica*, Aquinas says that bodies have a tendency to sink as well as to rise whereby their places are determined. "The pull from the higher worlds makes itself felt through 'levitation', and the pull from the lower world is felt as 'gravity', according to the quality of the past earthly life. The soul then follows, as it were, the magnetic pull from that supersensible region to which it feels akin, either 'gravitating' or 'levitating' as the case may be."[2]

The description by Thomas Aquinas is remarkably consistent with the operation of the Law of Gravitation as outlined above. We should also note that the process described by Thomas Aquinas implies the working of the Law of Attraction of Homogeneous Species.

The joint working of the Law of Gravitation and the Law of Attraction of Homogeneous Species determines where we find ourselves after physical death; God does not personally intervene to assign us to particular places. Our inner qualities at the time of departure activate the Laws. Thus, we see that with His immutable laws, God ensures that individuals judge themselves; we are always the architects of our own fates, even after physical death. We place ourselves in the Regions of Darkness and Damnation or in the Regions of Light and Paradise.

---

[2] Summa Theologica, Suppl. 69.2. Cited by Rudolf Frieling, *Christianity and Reincarnation*, Edinburgh, Floris Books, 1977, pp. 52-53

CHAPTER SEVEN

The Law of Balance

The concept of balance is one with which most people are familiar. We instinctively sense that whatever is outofbalance is unsatisfactory or wrong. There is a problem whenever accounts cannot be balanced. We speak of "balanced diets", referring to the necessity to eat different kinds of food items in appropriate proportions to ensure good health. Breathing out is balanced with breathing in. The stars, planets, and other celestial bodies are maintained in their incessant motion along predictable paths through a "balance of forces".

These are all manifestations of a Primordial Law of Creation: the Law of Necessary Balance between Giving and Taking, or simply the Law of Balance, which may also be called the Law of Equilibrium. This Law permeates everything and its strict observance in human affairs is a precondition for harmony and peace.

For a better understanding let us consider more manifestations of the Law of Balance. Actions are balanced by reactions. Food intake is balanced by waste elimination; we have constipation and feel sick when there is poor digestion and, therefore, inadequate elimination of food wastes.

Endless work without rest is harmful; complete retirement from work, that is, endless rest, is equally harmful. If after retirement from employment, a person does absolutely nothing, the person will soon fall ill and die. We should engage ourselves in appropriate work until our very last day on earth. The matter of complete retirement from work has already been discussed with respect to the Law of Movement.

In our breathing we are compelled to observe the Law of Balance; exhaling is balanced with inhaling. Many people have recognized how important good breathing is for the maintenance of radiant health, and so there are people who teach the art of correct breathing. The simple key is to breathe out properly; with proper exhalation, proper inhalation automatically follows, in accordance with the Law of Balance.

The balance, an instrument for weighing, is popularly used as a symbol of the judiciary and earthly justice. This symbolism is a good one; for it is correct to say that where there is no balance, there can be no justice.

THE LAW OF BALANCE 109

Indeed, the Law of Balance between Giving and Taking reflects Justice, which is an attribute of the Creator.

The Law of Balance is fundamental in all human relationships, whether interpersonal, between groups, or among nations. There must be balance in marriage, in the relationship between children and parents, between the employer and the employee, between the leader and the follower. In all these situations, harmony, peace, and progress are achieved only when giving and taking are appropriately balanced.

Pierre de Boisguilbert (1646-1714), a French economist, came to the recognition of the utmost importance of balance more than three centuries ago. He wrote: "Only equilibrium (balance) can save everyone; and nature alone, to repeat, can achieve this." I suppose he implied that there must be constant and conscious volition on the part of everyone to understand the requirements of balance and to adjust to them in every sphere of endeavour, not only in economic matters.

The conceptions of giving and of taking as they apply in each situation must, of course, be correctly understood. Thus, the desire of a parent to have a child must be balanced with the duty to take care of the child. The protection which adults offer children must be balanced by the obligation of children to respect adults. And the child, as soon as it is physically able to do so, should be made to contribute something to the home to balance the parental care it receives. The contribution would take the form appropriate to the child's circumstance; it could be running errands around the house, helping with minor chores, etc.

Among other things, the above examples suggest that the Law of Balance does not necessarily imply quantitative equivalence; nor does it require that one should give back the same kind of thing that one received. In some circumstances, the requirements of balance are met when the receiver shows genuine and heartfelt gratitude, offers prayer for the giver, or gives some good advice. Thus, everybody, rich or poor, is able to fulfil the demands of the Law of Balance. Most of us do not obey the Law only because of our individual weaknesses, such as presumption, thoughtlessness, and other manifestations of spiritual immaturity.

It also follows from the above that we really do not need to ponder what and how much we should give in return for whatever we receive. We should be guided by our intuition and simply give as much as we can of what we have. And even the poorest can offer heartfelt prayers, gratitude and a kind look to the giver. In this and in all matters, genuineness of one's volition and intentions and the purity of one's heart are always the essential considerations from the standpoint of the Laws of Creation.

The Law of Balance is reflected in the way the human being is constituted physically as well as spiritually. As an example: human beings are endowed with the *intellect* so that in every life on earth they have a *counterpoise pulling downwards* to balance the upward-striving *spirituality*. The intellect was given to us to prevent us as human spirits from constantly floating in spiritual heights to the detriment of our tasks on earth.

The intellect is generally to facilitate life on earth for us human beings who, as spirits, are actually aliens on earth. It is intended to anchor on earth the higher values that are an inherent quality of the spirit and thereby to ensure that those values make visible impact in the material world. It should act as the handyman of the living spirit, whose urges and decisions it should help to carry out. The intellect is designed to be the tool and the servant of the spirit. Sadly, the intellect has become over-cultivated and no longer serves as the tool of the spirit. Thus, the higher values of the spirit are only rarely reflected in the activities of human beings on earth.

Giving Comes First

In the Law of Balance between Giving and Taking, giving always ranks first. We can readily understand that this must be so on account of the Law of Reciprocal Action. Each time we give, we are sowing. And we know that each seed we sow will, at the appropriate time, return to us in multiples of the seeds of the same kind.

On the other hand, the seed we take or receive is like a harvest; once we have eaten it, that is the end of it. A cycle is closed with each receiving, whereas we start a new cycle whenever we give. Therefore, because we stand to gain multiples of whatever we give, it is always better, more blessed, to give than to receive.

In the Bible, Apostle Paul is reported to have addressed the matter of giving and receiving in his Farewell Speech to the Elders of

THE LAW OF BALANCE

Ephesus. He remarked that he had not sought to receive money or clothing from anyone but had worked hard to obtain all his needs as well as the needs of his companions. He urged his audience to support the weak and to remember the following words of the Lord Jesus: "It is more blessed to give than to receive." Some versions of the Bible render the statement attributed to Jesus as "There is more happiness in giving than in receiving." Below are the relevant verses in two versions of the Bible:

> I coveted no one's silver or gold or clothing. You know for yourselves that I worked with my own hands to support myself and my companions. In all this I have given you an example that by such work we must support the weak, remembering the words of the Lord Jesus, for he himself said, *"It is more blessed to give than to receive."* (Acts 20:33-35, New Revised Standard Version, *italics added*).

> I have never asked anyone for money or clothes; you know for yourselves that these hands of mine earned enough to meet my needs and those of my companions. By every means I have shown you that we must exert ourselves in this

way to support the weak, remembering the words of the Lord Jesus, who himself said, *"There is more happiness in giving than in receiving."* (Acts 20:33-35, New Jerusalem Bible, *italics added*).

It should be noted that both renderings of the statement attributed to Jesus indicate that giving ranks first. The fact that Apostle Paul relied on his own personal labour and resources to carry out his extensive and arduous mission is highly remarkable; it contrasts sharply with the expectations and exploitative practices of some contemporary religious leaders.

In line with what Jesus Christ said, the Koran has much to say about giving:

> And be steadfast in prayer
> And regular in charity
> And whatever good
> Ye send forth for your souls
> Before you, ye shall find it
> With Allah: for Allah sees
> Well all that ye do (Sura II:110, Yusuf Ali Version, italics mine)
> The parable of those who spend their substance
> In the way of Allah is that of a grain or corn: it groweth

Seven ears, and each ear
Hath a hundred grains (Sura II: 261,
Yusuf Ali Version).

These passages and many more in the Koran are the basis of the prominence of alms-giving (Zakat) in Islam. Nobody is expected to indulge in onesided taking, whereas everybody is urged to give. Hence whenever there is an opportunity to give, we should grab it joyfully. But we must always remember that we should give out of love, out of a genuine desire to help in the manner most beneficial to the recipient. Let us also note that love is implied in the Law of Reciprocal Action, in that the Law ensures that from a grain we harvest "a hundred grains" (Sura II: 261).

What we get in return for what we give does not depend on the recipient — whether or not he deserves it, whether or not he is grateful or ungrateful, whether or not he is even aware of the help are all unimportant. What was said about the attitude toward the suffering in connection with the Law of Reciprocal Action also applies here exactly. We get the reward due to us and when it is due *only* in accordance with the Primordial Laws of Creation.

And finally, we should bear in mind the fact that the principle is the same whether the giver or receiver is an individual, a group, or a nation. This has implications for public policy at all levels, including national and international levels. If, for example, every recipient nation gives something in return, a system of dynamic exchange would emerge, thus promoting global development, mutual respect, and happiness for all. And every recipient nation can give something in return — be it only genuine gratitude and appreciative conduct.

Receiving is Necessary

Let us be reminded that the Law of Balance, like all the Laws of Creation, is all-embracing; it applies to all aspects of life — spiritual as well as physical and material. Therefore, we should not overemphasize the earthly and physical aspects of the Law nor should we think of it only in connection with the relationships among us human beings. Moreover, human beings and all other creatures can exist only through the benevolence of the Creator. No human being can exist for more than a few minutes without taking in (receiving) air, which we take for granted. Not only do we not show gratitude for it, we sometimes pollute the air unapologetically.

The point is that we are all receivers/takers and, to varying degrees, ungrateful ones for that matter. Therefore, there is no basis to look down on anyone (such as a street beggar) who is obliged to receive from others. In other words, while it is the case that it is more blessed to give than to take, it does not mean that taking or receiving is wrong. But, of course, every taker must strive to give, in the sense already indicated above.

In this connection, let us reflect on the following statement of Abd-ru-shin, the author of The Grail Message:

> As I have already said, being spiritual man always and only takes as a guest what has already been laid upon the table of this Creation by the substantiate beings. Unfortunately he takes it in a wilful and demanding manner, instead of showing joyful gratitude and looking reverently up to Him Who proffers all this. And in this he must now change! (*In the Light of Truth, The Grail Message*, Volume III, Lecture: "The Cycle of Radiations").

A most important consideration in our time is that, under the increased spiritual power now pouring into Creation, all past imbalances are being forcibly corrected. And in future, it will not be possible to sustain such deviations from the Law of Balance.

Indeed, the existing structural problems in the global and national economies can be explained largely in terms of humankind's disregard for the Law of Balance; the widespread push for structural adjustment programs around the world is part of the process of forcible restoration of appropriate balance.

We can make the process of restructuring much less painful by identifying areas of imbalance and making conscious and voluntary efforts to make amends, whether it is in international trade, in industrial relations, in setting prices for goods and services, in the financial system including exchange rates, or in any other economic activity. However, in doing so we must be ever mindful of the fact that the purpose of human existence is spiritual; humankind's spiritual goal should be the primary focus.

But it is not only economies that need restructuring. We should strive for balance in all human activities and human relationships. Thus, the ongoing world democratic revolution is also connected with the restoring of balance in the exercise of national and international power — political, economic and social power. In particular, we must strike the right balance between the material and the spiritual in our individual lives. Today, humanity is a technological giant but remains a spiritual midget. World events remind us that we must now consciously tilt the balance in favour of true spirituality, or else we will perish.

CHAPTER EIGHT
The Law of the Cycle

A Primordial Law of Creation called the Law of the Cycle ensures that, in the World of Matter, whatever has a beginning must have an end and that the end must always flow back into the beginning. This Law is closely similar to the Law of Reciprocal Action; for each time we reap the seed of what we planted, a cycle is closed. Nature provides many examples.

The changing seasons give us a conception of cycle. In Spring, there is an awakening in nature with fresh growth. This is followed by development and maturing in Summer and then a ripening and harvest in Autumn. A period of rest and recuperation follows in Winter after which Spring returns and another cycle begins. This cycle of coming into existence and passing away is without end. However, every phase of the cycle, every happening during the cycle does have an end; for example, each season has an end.

The blood circulation in the human body illustrates the Law of the Cycle. Systemic circulation carries oxygenated blood from the left ventricle of the heart to all the organs of the body passing through the arteries to the capillaries in the tissues of the body. From the tissue capillaries, the deoxygenated blood returns through a system of veins to the right atrium of the heart. The pulmonary circulation is a short loop that takes up the deoxygenated blood from the heart to the lungs where the blood is re-oxygenated and returned to the heart for another round of circulation.

Water, which as vapour rises from the ocean into the atmosphere, returns from there in liquid (rain) or solid form (hail or snow) directly to the ocean or to dry land, and finds its way back into the ocean. And the cycle continues.

Our earth and the entire World of Matter (which includes the Ethereal World, the so-called Beyond) had a beginning and will come to an end, in obedience to this Law of the Cycle. The human spirit is subject to the Law of the Cycle. The cycle of some human actions carried out on earth must be closed on earth. For example, a perpetrator of an evil that is not atoned for before earthly death may be compelled to reincarnate to make amends and close the cycle of the evil action.

THE LAW OF THE CYCLE

And there is always the danger of further entanglements in a new earth-life, thereby delaying the ascent to Paradise.

The human spirit originated from the Spiritual Realm as an unconscious spirit germ (or spirit seed) and journeys to the World of Matter in which through appropriate experiencing it acquires consciousness, self-consciousness, and inner maturity. When it has matured fully, it returns automatically as a self-conscious spirit to its origin in the Spiritual Realm, in accordance with the Law of the Cycle. And as a consequence of its maturity, it becomes a full member of its particular community in the Spiritual Realm and can participate in the further development of Creation.

If a human spirit were to fail to achieve full maturity by the time the World of Matter is due to disintegrate, it would be caught up in the disintegrating process. The consciousness and self-consciousness that the human spirit had acquired would be destroyed; it would lose its personal "ego". It would be reverted to an unconscious spirit germ in an indescribably horrible and painful process. That is spiritual death, which is also called eternal damnation. However, in accordance with the Law of the Cycle, the spirit germ in its unconscious state would automatically be returned to its origin in the Spiritual Realm.

Consider: any animal that does not get out of a burning bush because it is indolent, inattentive, or fails to find an escape route gets burnt with the bush. So it is with the human spirit in the material parts of Creation. Human beings who, for whatever reasons, have not left the World of Matter by the time the part of the world in which they inhabit must come to an end will suffer disintegration, spiritual death. In His Omniscience and Love, God affords human beings various helps, which rightly used would ensure that we do not suffer the fate of spiritual death but rather are able to return to the Spiritual Realm as fully self-conscious mature human spirits able to participate in the further development of Creation.

CHAPTER NINE
Concluding Remarks

A New Dawn Approaches

In our era, many cycles are coming to a close for individuals as well as for groups. In addition, a tremendous cosmic cycle is coming to a close. Among the cycles that are closing are those of events connected with the life and mission of Jesus, the Son of God. In the process, the distortions and misinterpretations of His teachings are brought to light. His true mission is explained and His true teachings are clarified and extended in fulfilment of His promise of the coming of the Spirit of Truth.

Similarly, the earth-lives and true teachings of prominent past truth-bringers, including but not limited to Hjalfdar, Krishna, Zoroaster, Lao-Tse, Buddha, and Mohammed are revealed. All these are acts of Grace; they provide final opportunities for accelerated spiritual maturing to those who listen and act as desired by Jesus and these other truth-bringers.

There is acceleration everywhere. All sorts of events are unfolding with a rapidity hitherto unknown. Among other consequences, there is a shortening of the cycle of sowing and reaping for everyone and for every group, including nation-states. It is for this reason that we are witnessing an astounding multiplicity and convergence of bewildering events in political, economic, social, spiritual and other spheres of life, human-made as well as natural (such as earthquakes, volcanic eruptions, etc.). But the Primordial Laws of Creation remain immutable and are strengthened in their automatic activity.

These events are associated with the World Judgment and are a clarion call to rethink the meaning of life and to pay much greater attention to the Will of God that manifests in the Primordial Laws of Creation.

The World Judgment will usher in the new kingdom, the Kingdom of God on earth and with it a new generation. It will come about through forcible remodelling of all that is distorted, a process which is already taking place. All that is wrong, false and evil must run itself to death propelled by the invincible power and force of the Light.

The process is in complete accordance with the immutable Primordial Laws. But the increasing power of the Light compels adjustment to them. As stated in the Grail Message:

> The threads of all the Divine Laws in Creation are being charged with increased energy, so that they become powerfully taut. This enormous tension causes them to spring back into their original position. What is tangled and knotted is thereby disentangled, so suddenly and irresistibly that everything that cannot still adapt itself to the right position in Creation is simply torn down in this process.
>
> Whatever it may be, whether plant or animal, whether mountains, streams, countries, states or man himself, all will collapse that cannot prove itself at the last moment to be genuine and willed by God! (*In the Light of Truth, The Grail Message*, Volume I, Lecture: "Submission").

The Primordial Laws and the Equal-Armed Cross in the Ring

Dr. Richard Steinpach (1917-1992) was an Austrian lawyer, philosopher, and a prolific author of books and essays. As an adherent of Abd-ru-shin's work, *In the Light of Truth, The Grail Message*, Dr. Steinpach gave very many lectures to audiences in many cities in Germany, Austria, and Switzerland between 1979 and 1991. Some of the lectures were subsequently published as books. One of such books, originally issued in German, has been published in two English-language editions: "*Why does God allow such things···*" was published in 1991 in Germany and another version was published in the United States in 1995 as "*How Can God Allow Such Things?*"

In the course of explaining how it is that each person is truly the architect of his/her own fate, Dr. Steinpach discusses the Primordial Laws of Creation as well as reincarnation. He summarized the Laws and provided a way by which to remember them (a mnemonic). He stated this mnemonic, or formula to facilitate remembrance, as follows:

> There is the *Law of Gravity*. It works from above downwards as it were; picture it simply as a **vertical line**.

The Law of Attraction of Homogeneous Species unites on the same plane those things that correspond to each other; hence picture it as a **horizontal line**. Finally there is the *Law of Reciprocal Action*, which links beginning and end in the closing of the cycle; that would be consistent with a **circle**. Picture as a symbol an **equal-armed cross** in a ring, and you have before your eyes the three incontestable Primordial Laws of Creation, the all-creating Living Truth in the ancient symbol of faith.

And for their part, these three basic Laws are nothing but forms of activity of one single cause: *movement*. Movement brought about by the sustaining Radiation Pressure of God. Indeed, everything in Creation is movement, from the orbit of the planets to the atoms; there is no standstill anywhere. This movement demands that we go with it, for only in movement is there life – just think of our heartbeat.[1]

The equal-armed cross in the ring is the image of the Living Truth *within* Creation. It

---
[1] Richard Steinpach, *Why does God allow such things* ···Stuttgart, Stiftung Gralsbotschaft Publishing Co., 1991, pp. 36-37; see also Richard Steinpach, *How Can God Allow Such Things?* Gambier, Ohio, Grail Foundation Press, 1995, pp. 31-32.

is quite different from the crosses used by various Christian denominations to symbolize the crucifixion of Jesus Christ. The equal-armed cross in the ring is a symbol to remind us human spirits as creatures in Creation that we must adjust ourselves in everything and in every way to the Primordial Laws of Creation.

INDEX

A
Abd-ru-shin, 7, 62
Abilities, 25, 39-40
Abortion, 51-52
Acceleration of Events, 125-127
Accountability, 65-66
Acknowledging One's Guilt, 82, 83-84, 90
Acts of the Apostles, 113, 114
Adaptation, 24-25
Adjustment to the Laws, 1-3, 9, 126-127
Alpha and Omega of Spiritual Knowledge, 7
Analogies, 1-2, 7-8, 11, 124
Angels and Archangels, 66-67
Anger, Righteous, 97-98
Aquinas, Thomas, 104-105
Arbitrariness and Forgiveness, 85-86
Astral Model, 52
Attitude to the Suffering, 77-80
Attraction, genuine, 45
Authority and Responsibility, 65-66

B
Balance
    As symbol of Judiciary, 108-109
    Between work and rest, 108
    Forcible restructuring of balance, 118-119, 126-127
    Principle of, 107
    see also Law of Balance
Basic Writings of Bertrand Russell, The, 10, 29
Beggars, 117
Beliefs and Belief Systems, 25-26, Questionable Beliefs, 26-29
Bernhardt, Oskar Ernst, 6
Beyond, The, 47-48
Bible see individual books, e.g. *Matthew*
Blood Circulation, 121-122
Blotting Out Sins, 81-82
Bodies, Non-Physical, 101-102
Boisguilbert, Pierre de, 109
Brain, 25
Breathing, 107, 108
Buddha, 125

C
Catastrophe, 126-127
Cerebellum, 25
Cerebrum, 25
Children and their Families, 50-53
Christian and Reincarnation, The, 75
Christianity and Reincarnation, 105
Church Confessions, 91-93
Climate Change, 69
Commandments, 12
Comprehensive Nature of the Laws, 6
Computer Programs, 7-8
Conception, 50
Conviction, 99
Cosmology, 5-6, 8-9
Creation, Structure of, 8-9
Cross of Crucifixion, 129
Cross of Truth, 128-130
Culture, 32
Cycle, Concept of, 121
Cycle of Sowing and Reaping, 121
Cynicism, 54-56

D

Death-Bed Repentance, 98-99
Deism, 63
Dementia, 30
Denonn, Lester E., 10, 29
Desires, 10
Deuteronomy, 63
Disintegration, 124
Distrust, 54-56
Divine Realm, 6
Doctrines, 25-29
Donations, 72
Dred Scott v. Sandford, 18

E

Earthly Interactions, 47-48
Economies, Structural Problems, 118-119
Egalitarianism, 34-41
Egner, Robert E., 10, 29
Environment, 69
Ephesus, Elders of, 112-114
Equal-Armed Cross, 128-130
Equalitarianism *see* Egalitarianism
Equilibrium *see* Balance
Equipment Manuals, 1-2
Equity *see* Inequality and Equity
Eternal Laws *see* Primordial Laws
Ethereal Bodies, 101-102
Ethnicity and Ethnic Relations, 49
Evil, 54-56, 69, 86-87, 102
Exercise, 24

F

Families, 50-53
Fate, 99, 105
Faults, Recognition of, 54-59
Forgiveness, 81-99
    And Reincarnation, 98-99
    Who can forgive? 89-93
Free Will, 9, 46, 64-70
Freedom, 68
Frieling, Rudolf, 105

G

Gate Opens, A, 101
Germany, 19-20
Giving and Taking, 109-111
    Giving comes first, 112-116
    Receiving is necessary, 116-117
    See also Law of Balance
Glories *see* Past Glories
Goals, 33
God's Will and the Primordial Laws, 1-3, 5, 12-14
Gossips, 54-56
Grail Message *see In the Light of Truth, The Grail Message*
Gratitude, 116, 117
Gravitation *see* Law of Gravitation
Greed, 102-103
Guests in Creation, 117

H

Happiness, 3, 33, 77
Harmony, 3,
Health, 24, 30
Heaviness, Causes, 102-103
Hell, 46
Heredity, 52-53
Hitler, Adolf, 19
Hjalfdar, 125
Holy Spirit, sins against, 93-96

*How Can God Allow Such
    Things?* 128, 129
Human-Made Laws, Contrasted
    with the Primordial Laws,
    16-21
Human Purpose, 33, 123-124
Human Relationships, 108,
    109-110

I

Ignorance, not an excuse, 14
*In the Light of Truth, The Grail
    Message*, 7, 13, 21, 55, 63,
    84, 117, 126
Incarnation, 50-53
Indolence, 29, 32, 33
Indulgence, 33
Inequality and Equity, 34-41
Intellect and Spirit, 25, 67, 111-
    112
Intellectual Giants, 25, 119
Intervals between Sowing and
    Reaping, 73-75
Isaiah, The Book of, 81-82

J

Jesus
    And sins against the Holy
        Spirit, 94-96
    And the Primordial Laws, 14,
        34-41, 103-104
    Clarification of His
        Teachings, 34-39,
        40-41, 125
    On mother and brothers, 49
    Post-Resurrection
        Appearance, 91
    Temptation of, 103-104
John, Gospel According to, 91
Joyful Activity, 33

Judas Iscariot, 91
Judges, their spiritual responsi-
    bility, 65-66
Judging, 56-57, 72, 74
Judiciary, 108-109
Justice, 18-20,
    And Love, 21
    And Purity, 21

K

Karma see Mission Karma
Koran, 114-115
Knight, Polishing and Shining the
    Armour of a Sick Night, 11
Knowledge, the Imperative of
    Spiritual Knowledge, 1-3,
    7, 11
Krishna, 125

L

Lampe, Stephen M., 9, 75
Lao-Tse, 125
Law of Attraction of Homoge-
    neous Species, 21, 43-59, 72,
    83, 103
Law of Balance, 21, 107-119
Law of Gravitation, 21, 46,
    101-105
Law of Love as the One Basic
    Law, 20-21
Law of Movement, 21, 23-41
Law of Reciprocal Action, 21, 53,
    61-80, 121
Law of Sowing and Reaping *see*
    Law of Reciprocal Action
Law of Spiritual Gravity *see* Law
    of Gravitation
Law of the Cycle, 21, 121-124,
    125
Legality and Morality, 18-21

Levitation, 104
Liars, 59
Life After Death, 25, 33, 47-48, 101-103
Lord's Prayer, The, 85, 96
Love as the One Basic Law, 20-21
  Love in the Law of Reciprocal Action, 75-77
Luke, Gospel According to, 34-35, 36

M

Magnets, Opposite Poles, 44-45
Man-Made Laws *see* Human-Made Laws
Manual for Creation, 1-2
Manufacturers, 1
Mark, Gospel According to, 34-35, 85, 94, 96, 97
Marriage and Morals, 10
Matthew, Gospel According to, 34-36, 49, 94, 95
McLean, Justice John, 18
Mirrors into the inner being, 54-60
Mission Karma, 78-80
Mnemonic, 128-129
Mohammed, Prophet, 125
Money, Bad one drives out good one, 43
Money-Changers in the Temple, 97-98
Morality and Legality, 18-20
Mosaic Laws, 14
Motion Characterizes Creation, 23-24
  see also Law of Movement
Motives, 17, 72

N-O

Natural Disasters, 69
Natural Law, 20
Nazi Laws, 19-20
Neighbours, Knowing Ourselves through, 56-59
Nuremberg Anti-Semitic Legislation, 19
Offenders, Actions Against, 97-98
Official Decisions and Personal Responsibility, 65-66
Omniscience at Work, 54-56; 56-59, 124
Opportunities, 39-40

P-Q

Parables, 34-39
  Lessons, 39
  Of the Pounds (or Gold Coins), 36, 37-38
  Of the Prodigal Son, 84
  Of the Sower, 35-36
  Of the Talents, 36-37
Paradise, 53, 68, 80, 102, 105, 123
Past and Present, 31
Past Glories, 31
Paul the Apostle, Farewell to the Elders of Ephesus, 112-114
Penitent Thief on the Cross, 83
Perfection, 13, 16
Peter, Second Letter of, 23
Policy-Making *see* Public Policy
Poor, Dispossessing the Poor, 34-39
Popular Sayings, 17, 43
Pounds, Parable of the, 36, 37-38
Practice, 32
Priests and Forgiveness, 91-93

Primordial, Meaning of, 5
Primordial Laws
    General Characteristics, 1-3, 12-21
    Imperative to study them, 1-3
    Role of Invisible Beings, 63
        See also specific laws, e.g. Law of Gravitation
Procreation, 51
Prodigal Son, 84
Progress, Sustainable, 9-11
Prophets, 125
Proverbs and Primordial Laws, 17, 43
Public Policy, 2-3, 41, 68, 69, 107
Punishment, 83
Purity, 21
Purpose of Human Existence, 1-3, 33, 123-124
Quantum Physics, 15
Questions on the Natural Law, 20
Qur'an *see* Koran

R

Race and Race Relations, 49-50
Recompense *see* Vengeance and Recompense
Reformation and Forgiveness, 84
Reforming and Reforms, 10-11,
Reincarnation, 74-75, 98-99, 122-123
Religions, 2, 12
    and the Law of Movement, 25-29
    and the Law of Reciprocal Action, 61-63
Responsibility, 65-66
Rest In Peace (R.I.P.), 32-33
Retaliation *see* Vengeance

Retirement, 30-31, 108
Retrogression, 11
Rhythm, 30
Rice, Charles E., 20
Rich, Enriching the Rich, 34-39
Rigidity, 26-29
Russell, Bertrand, 9, 27, 28, 29

S

Science and the Primordial Laws, 14-16
Seasons, 121
Secrets of the kingdom of heaven, 40-41
Self-Knowledge, 54-60
Separation, stricter in the Beyond, 47-48
Simplicity of the Primordial Laws, 16-17
Slavery, 18-19
Sower, Parable of the, 35-36
Sowing, types of, 71-72
Sowing and Reaping *see* the Law of Reciprocal Action
Speck in our neighbour's eye, 56-59
Species, whole and split, 44-45
Spirit and Intellect, 25, 67, 111-112
Spirit Germs, 123
Spirit of Truth, 125
Spiritual Midgets, 25, 119
Spiritual Qualities, 48-50
Split Species, 44-45
Steinpach, Richard, 128, 129
Subsequent Creation, 8
Suffering, Attitude to, 77-78
Summa Theologica, 104, 105
Sustainable Progress, 9-11
Symbolic Redemption, 86-89

T

Taking *see* Giving and Taking
Talents, Parable of the, 36-37
Technological Giants, 25, 119
Thief on the Cross, 83
Thinking About God: Reflections on Conceptions and Misconceptions, 9
Thomas, Disciple, 91
Thoughts and Thought Forms, 17, 50, 53, 71, 82-83, 102-103
Traditions, 32
Tragedies, 77
Truth-Bringers, 125

U-V

U.S. Declaration of Independence, 18
U.S. Supreme Court, 18
Understanding, 10-11
Union of Split Parts, 45
Values, 26, 33
Vengeance and Recompense, 63, 70-71
Victims of Offence, Attitude of, 96-98
Vollmann, Herbert, 101

W-Z

Why Does God Allow Such Things···, 128, 129
Workaholism, 30
Works, include speech, 56
World Events, 10-11
World Judgment, 118, 126-127
World of Matter, 8-9
Zakat, 115
Zoroaster, 125

www.ingramcontent.com/pod-product-compliance
Lightning Source LLC
Chambersburg PA
CBHW060802050426
42449CB00008B/1497